Japanese Business in Canada

The Elusive Alliance

Japanese Business in Canada

The Elusive Alliance

Richard W. Wright

The Institute for Research on Public Policy /

L'Institut de recherches politiques

Legal Deposit Fourth Quarter
Bibliothèque nationale du Québec

Canadian Cataloguing in Publication Data
Wright, Richard W., 1939-
Japanese business in Canada

Bibliography: p.
ISBN 0-88645-005-5

1. Japan—Commerce—Canada. 2. Canada—Commerce—
Japan. 3. Investments, Japanese—Canada.
I. Institute for Research on Public Policy
II. Title.

HF1480.15.J3W75 1984   C84-090139-9   382.'0971'052

The Institute for Research on Public Policy/
L'Institut de recherches politiques
2149 Mackay Street, Montreal, Quebec H3G 2J2

Contents

Foreword

Direct overseas investment by Japanese corporations began to increase rapidly in the latter half of the 1970s, with the result that Japan has quickly become the fifth-largest foreign investor in the world. Although well behind the United States and the United Kingdom, the top two foreign investors, Japan will increasingly become an important source of new investment. The potential for further Japanese business investment in Canada is enormous, but for it to be realized, certain Canadian misconceptions must be removed. An awareness of the nature, the role, and the impact of Japanese investment in Canada is crucial for establishing sound policies relating to the growing Canada-Japan economic relationship.

Richard Wright's study fills the need of chronicling and analysing the Japanese business presence in Canada. It reveals several distinguishing characteristics of Japanese investment, which should help to allay some traditional Canadian concerns about foreign investment. Japanese investment is small in proportion to the total volume of Canada-Japan trade. The study shows that unlike other traditional foreign investors, who generally seek to gain direct control of affiliated companies in Canada, Japanese investors aim primarily to secure reliable flows of raw materials. Because the Japanese emphasis is on trade rather than on investment flows, a high proportion of Japanese investment is in the form of loans rather than equity, and the Japanese often take minority holdings or enter into joint ventures. The role of Japanese investment is thus a very different one from that which has been a source of concern about foreign ownership in Canada.

In view of existing trade friction, but of overall 'complementarity' between the two countries, the Institute hopes that this pioneering study will help to lay the groundwork for additional research into the broadening Canada-Japan relationship. The Institute is pleased to have had co-sponsorship for this project from the Japan Foundation of Tokyo.

Gordon Robertson
Past President and Fellow-in-Residence

June 1984

Avant-propos

Le rythme de l'investissement direct à l'étranger des sociétés japonaises s'est accéléré au cours de la deuxième partie des années 70, de sorte que le Japon est rapidement devenu le cinquième plus important investisseur international du monde. Bien qu'il se range toujours loin derrière les États-Unis et le Royaume-Uni, les deux plus importants investisseurs internationaux, le Japon est appelé à devenir une source de plus en plus importante de nouveaux placements. Les possibilités d'investissements commerciaux japonais au Canada sont énormes mais pour qu'elles se réalisent il faudra dissiper certains malentendus. Seule une connaissance de la nature, du rôle et des répercussions des investissements japonais au Canada peut garantir l'à-propos des mesures relatives aux rapports économiques de plus en plus étroits entre le Canada et le Japon.

Cette étude de Richard Wright comble le besoin de répertorier et d'analyser la présence commerciale japonaise au Canada. On y révèle certaines caractéristiques des investissements japonais qui devraient aider à apaiser quelques-unes des inquiétudes traditionnelles que nourrissent les Canadiens face aux investissements étrangers. L'investissement japonais ne représente qu'une faible proportion du commerce entre les deux pays. A la différence des autres investisseurs étrangers classiques, qui cherchent habituellement à diriger des sociétés affiliées au Canada, les investisseurs japonais cherchent surtout à s'assurer des approvisionnements stables en matières premières. Parce que les Japonais insistent davantage sur le commerce que sur le mouvement des capitaux, ils réalisent une forte proportion de leurs placements sous forme de prêts plutôt que de participation au capital et ils s'assurent souvent une participation minoritaires ou encore s'engagent dans des coentreprises. Le rôle de l'investissement japonais diffère de beaucoup de celui qui soulève toujours des inquiétudes au sujet de la propriété étrangère au Canada.

Compte tenu des relations commerciales tendues mais, néanmoins "complémentaires" entre les deux pays, l'Institut espère que cette étude qui en est une de pionnier jette les bases de recherches supplémentaires concernant l'évolution des relations entre le Canada et le Japon. L'Institut se félicite d'avoir obtenu le coparrainage de la Japan Foundation de Tokyo pour cette étude.

Ancien président,
Gordon Robertson

Juillet 1984

The Author

Richard W. Wright is Professor of International Business in the Faculty of Management, McGill University. He holds Bachelor's and Master's degrees from Dartmouth College and a Doctorate from Indiana University. Dr. Wright is active throughout the world in management training and business consulting. His publications include five books and numerous articles on finance, international business, and Japanese management. He has lived and worked in Japan for several periods.

Acknowledgements

This report is one of a series of studies examining the probable economic and social impacts of foreseeable technological changes in Canada. The project, directed by Zavis P. Zeman, was part of the Technology and Society Program of the Institute for Research on Public Policy. The co-operation and support of many organizations and individuals went into its making.

Appreciation is due first to the two organizations—one on each side of the Pacific—that joined in financing this project: The Institute for Research on Public Policy, in Canada, and the Japan Foundation, in Tokyo. The author hopes that those organizations will consider that their money was well spent.

The Japan External Trade Organization (JETRO) played a key role in the successful conduct of the research, by assisting in the planning of various stages and by providing introductions to the personnel of many Japanese companies. Particular appreciation is due to Mr. Tatsuo Fujimura, former Executive Director of the Japan Trade Center in Toronto, and to Mr. Mamoru Iwamoto and Mr. Robert Ulmer, of the same organization.

The research task would have been vastly more difficult had it not been for the co-operation of Statistics Canada personnel, many of whom went out of their way to locate and provide access to needed information. Thanks are due especially to Craig Gaston and Michel Bedard, of the Structural Analysis Division, who co-ordinated the flow of data from various divisions of Statistics Canada, and who patiently explained and ran the input-output models.

Essential to a project of this magnitude is competent research assistance. The author was particularly fortunate to have had the assistance of Tejbir Singh Phool, a final-year MBA student at McGill University, whose knowledge of econometrics and general research competence were invaluable. Major editorial and content assistance was provided by Ursula Kobel. Special thanks are due also to Robert Letovsky for screening published information and preparing summary drafts; to Margaret Lewis for her understanding and patience through countless draft revisions; and to Peter Campbell, Keith Hay, Richard Gottlieb, Gregor Guthrie, Robert Hoffman, and Frank Winser for their advice and guidance.

Finally, an enormous debt of gratitude is owed to the many corporate managers and public officials who gave so willingly of their valuable time to be interviewed in the course of the research. The author hopes that their views and opinions are fairly represented in the final text.

Summary

In recent years Canadians, long accustomed to the presence of United States (US) business within their country, have become more and more aware of the growing presence of a new business partner: Japan. The present study, the result of over eighteen months of research by the author in Canada and Japan, documents the place and impact of Japanese business in Canada.

The Japanese presence is the source of a powerful dilemma for many Canadians. They see, on the one hand, important potential benefits to Canada, the result of an infusion of Japanese capital, skills, products and purchase contracts. But at the same time, Canadians viewing the export of Canadian raw materials to Japan and the import of Japanese manufactured products to Canada ask—rightly—just what benefits all of this exchange brings to Canada. Even more basically, wary Canadians wonder whether the growing Japanese business presence in Canada will, in the long run, merely substitute a new foreign master for a traditional one. Very little substantial evidence is available on which to base intelligent judgements about the place of Japanese business in Canada.

Canadian-Japanese Business: An Overview

Trade between Canada and Japan has grown dramatically in recent years, both in value and in terms of its importance to the two countries. By 1982 the volume of Canada-Japan trade had reached over $8 billion. On the surface, the trade relationship appears satisfactory to Canadians: the overall balance is consistently in Canada's favour. But Canadians have reasons for apprehension concerning both short-term developments and underlying structural characteristics. The size of the Canadian surplus on bilateral trade has shrunk substantially since 1979, both because of a slow-down of growth in Japanese demand for Canadian raw materials, and because of a dramatic increase in the import of Japanese autos which compete directly with a depressed domestic auto industry.

This immediate crisis is only one manifestation of a more fundamental qualitative imbalance in trade between the two countries: Canadian exports to Japan are mainly raw materials and commodities, whereas imports from Japan are almost exclusively manufactured products. This qualitative trade imbalance leaves Canada in the position of a less-developed country in relation to Japan, and the situation appears to be deteriorating, rather than improving. Mistrust and acrimony are bound to grow unless the Japanese take significant steps to arrange for more processing of raw materials before they leave Canada; to have more auto parts and other manufactured components produced in Canada; and to impose more orderly control on exports to Canada of Japanese-manufactured products which threaten to displace existing Canadian industries. These are all feasible steps which the Japanese could take at minimal cost to themselves.

Private direct investment between Canada and Japan is small, relative to the growth of trade and to the size of the domestic economies involved. Japanese investment in Canada has been growing rapidly and now exceeds $1 billion, but it still remains less than 1 per cent of total foreign investment in Canada.

Unlike other investors, who generally seek to gain direct control of affiliated companies in Canada, Japanese investors aim primarily to secure reliable flows of raw materials to Japan and to facilitate the export sale of products manufactured in Japan. As a consequence, Japanese investment in Canada has unique characteristics: it is directed mainly into natural resources and merchandising, rather than manufacturing; it emphasizes long-term loans and minority equity positions, rather than attempting to gain control; and it flows largely to western Canada, rather than to the country's industrial heartland. In reflecting willingness to provide needed financing and to open markets without seeking to gain control, the Japanese aims seem compatible with Canada's stated objective of welcoming foreign participation which does not threaten its own national economic sovereignty. The problem is that only a very small portion of Japanese investment is directed towards manufacturing or processing activities which would maximize domestic job creation and value added. It is time, in the view of many Canadians, for the Japanese to become more willing to move some of their processing and manufacturing to the production sites of the resources they use, instead of their just moving energy and raw materials to the site of Japanese industry.

Japanese Business in Canada

Japanese business firms enter Canada for a variety of purposes, and their involvement takes many forms. This study classifies and discusses their activities in five categories:

• Energy and resources
• Merchandising
• Trade
• Manufacturing
• Services.

All known Canadian businesses with at least $10 000 assets or $5 000 annual sales, which are controlled to the extent of at least 50 per cent from Japan, as well as most such firms with 20-49 per cent Japanese control, have been analysed for their impact on the Canadian economy. The 160 firms included in these categories, directly employed a total of 13 419 people in Canada as of the end of 1981. The largest employment group was manufacturing (4667), followed closely by merchandising (4029) and resources (3390). If, however, all 2841 forestry-products employees and 155 rapeseed-oil employees were categorized under resources, rather than in the manufacturing classification used here, then the resource companies would constitute by far the largest group of employers with 6386 employees, or 47.6 per cent of the total, with manufacturing a distant third at 1671 employees or 12.5 per cent of the total.

Geographically, British Columbia accounts for by far the largest amount of direct employment in firms with significant Japanese participation; these firms employ 5960 people or 44.4 per cent of the national total. Although most of the British Columbia employment is in the resource industries, there is also substantial employment generated there in merchandising, trading, and manufacturing (assuming forestry products as manufacturing). The second-largest province of direct employment is Ontario, with 4247 employees, where most of the merchandising companies and banks are located. Employment in Quebec, with 1174 employees, is diversified among merchandising, trading and manufacturing. Nearly all of the Maritimes employment, covering 1230 employees, is generated by forestry (pulp) manufacturing in New Brunswick. Japanese businesses employ about 400 people in Alberta, mostly in the raising of cattle and the growing of rapeseed, and an equal number in Manitoba, who are almost all occupied in merchandising. Direct Japanese-controlled employment is virtually nil in Newfoundland, Nova Scotia, Prince Edward Island, Saskatchewan, and the Territories.

Direct-employment figures for each of the five main categories were compiled from a combination of published sources and personal interviews. Estimates of direct wages and salaries, and of direct value added, were computed from the Statistics Canada National Input-Output Model, using average Canadian ratios for wages and output per employee for each of the activities specified.

According to these estimates, the Japanese companies paid out gross wages and salaries of $225.7 million in Canada in 1981; 44 per cent of this amount was earned in the manufacturing sector, including the manufacture of forest products. The total direct value added by the same companies was $387.6 million, mainly in resource activities, which accounted for 43 per cent and manufacturing, which accounted for 34 per cent.

Economic Impact

While the figures given above represent the *direct* measurable effects of Japanese companies in Canada, these direct inputs stimulate, in turn, further production of goods and services as the employees and suppliers of the Japanese firms spend the incomes they have received. Thus, the initial direct demand created by the Japanese companies induces additional, indirect production and value added throughout other sectors of the economy. The full economic impact of these companies is best represented as a combination of direct and induced effects.

Employing the patterns of direct demand and the nature of the activities involved, Statistics Canada input-output models were used to simulate the economic impact of Japanese businesses in Canada. The results provide estimates both of the total employment and value-added impact for each of the groups, which are distributed among forty economic sectors, and of the distribution of employment and value-added impact by province.

The simulation results indicate that some 36 000-40 000 jobs in Canada are associated with Japanese business activity, as is some $1.2 billion of the gross domestic product (GDP). In proportion to the overall economy, these numbers may seem small. The total employment associated with Japanese business, for example, represents less than 1 per cent of the Canadian labour force. But the effects are significant. In the recent recessionary environment, while governments in Canada have expended enormous financial resources in attempts to create jobs and stimulate domestic production, Japanese companies are generating thousands of jobs and more than $1 billion-worth of annual domestic output at virtually no direct cost to the taxpayer. This is not to say that the benefits of this achievement are free of cost: there are, of course, associated outflows of natural resources and dividends, and some surrender of domestic economic control. But the nature of Japanese investment is such that the financial cost and loss of control are minimal.

The geographic distribution of the benefits derived from this Japanese business activity is also highly significant. As expected, the simulation results show total value added to be highest in western Canada, especially in British Columbia, where 60 per cent of the national total is generated. But the employment benefits are spread much more widely: 53 per cent is generated in eastern Canada, mainly in Ontario and Quebec, and 47 per cent in the Prairie and Western provinces, chiefly British Columbia. Thus, while the immediate impact of Japanese business activity in Canada appears to be highly concentrated, the derived benefits are distributed much more evenly across the country. The widespread distribution of benefits revealed by this analysis is a highly significant feature of the Japanese business presence that is not widely recognized by Canadians, who tend to focus only on the more visible (and highly concentrated) immediate effects.

Intangible Effects

The Japanese business presence has other far-reaching influences, which are more difficult to quantify. Considered in turn are the role of Japanese trading companies and the function of banks, project financing, purchase agreements, and technology and management transfer.

Trading Companies

The full economic importance of the Japanese trading companies extends far more widely than their impact on direct employment and consumption of goods and services. With their ample financial resources and their vast global information and communications networks, these companies play a key role in generating trade and stimulating investments in Canada. About 65 per cent of the volume of trading companies involves exports to Japan, mainly of raw materials. Twenty-six per cent consists of imports from Japan, and the remaining 9 per cent represents trade between Canada and countries other than Japan. Together, the nine general trading companies in Canada handled nearly *$5 billion*-worth of Canadian trade in 1980, accounting for 71 per cent of all Canadian exports to Japan and 41 per cent of Canada's imports from Japan. In addition to their bilateral activities, the trading companies handled $256 million-worth of Canadian exports to third countries, and $156 million-worth of third-country imports into Canada.

These same companies had invested the equivalent of US $179 million in Canada as of 1981, that is, 20 per cent of all Japanese investment in Canada. More important, by means of joint ventures, they have served as the key promoters and catalysts in drawing investments by other Japanese companies to Canada. Their impact thus extends well beyond their own immediate investment positions.

Banks

Despite their former inability to conduct direct commercial banking functions, twelve Japanese banks had established in Canada representative offices which performed a variety of services. Moreover, revisions of the Canadian Bank Act, effective January 1981, have set the stage for a more direct and substantial involvement, chiefly in financing major resource projects and other wholesale commercial services.

Project Financing

While their direct impact on Canada's resources sector is small, the Japanese play an exceedingly important indirect role in providing loan financing and purchase contracts essential to the viability of some of Canada's most ambitious megaprojects. Although the full impact of such indirect participation cannot be measured precisely, it constitutes probably the most substantial and far-reaching benefit to Canadians of any facet of the Japanese business presence.

Japanese firms are discouraged by Canada's National Energy Policy from participating directly in major petroleum projects and from exporting Canadian oil or gas until such time as Canada achieves energy self-sufficiency. Nevertheless, it is in Japan's interest to assist Canadians to explore and develop potential new oil and gas sources: if Canada produces more than enough of these resources to satisfy its domestic needs, then both Canadians and Japanese can gain by exporting some of the surplus to Japan. Even if oil export is not permitted, new oil discoveries in Canada would tend to reduce pressure in the world market, thus benefitting Japan. With this end in mind, the Japanese have committed large amounts of loan financing, often at extremely favourable rates of interest and without guarantee of repayment, to Canadian petroleum projects in the Arctic and in Alberta tar sands. In doing so without any assurance of the projects' success or of governmental approval to export oil, even if they are successful, the Japanese are also sharing significantly in the risks involved.

Purchase Agreements

The large capital investments required to exploit many of Canada's natural resources, particularly in coal, cannot be made without firm guarantees of sustained demand. While some demand for Canadian coal exists in smaller Asian and Latin American countries, by far the largest potential export market is Japan.

In several existing coal-mining operations, mostly in southern British Columbia, Japanese companies hold minority equity positions, and in some others they provide loans. But common to all operations in which they participate is the existence of long-term purchase contracts, often running up to fifteen years' duration, for the sale of output to Japanese firms. It is the purchase contracts, more than the actual financing provided, which ensure the viability of the mines.

Technology and Management

This research suggests that aside from a small handful of examples, Canada has received very little to date in the way of technology transfer from Japan. This probably is not surprising, as the focus of Japanese attention in Canada is on the extraction and processing of natural resources, activities in which Japan has only limited first-hand experience. It is likely that Japanese technology input will be more substantial in some of the high-technology resource-based projects, such as the production of liquified natural gas and the construction of petrochemical complexes that are planned for the future.

In general, the Japanese business presence in Canada seems to have had negligible influence on management practices. The management of most Japanese business affiliates in Canada is similar to that of comparable Canadian-owned businesses. One reason for this is that the effects of Japanese management practices are most visible in manufacturing operations, and the extent of Japanese manufacturing investment in Canada is insignificant. Japanese managers interviewed in the course of producing this research also cited the influence of Canadian labour unions as a major obstacle to their attempts to transfer management methods. Traditional Japanese management practices, which are based on open, direct communication between management and workers and on their common values, may be largely unworkable in Canada, given the militancy and perceived rigidity of Canadian unions.

The Elusive Alliance: A Personal Conclusion

During more than eighteen months of work on the present report, the author has held discussions with literally hundreds of individuals, both Japanese and Canadian. Two conclusions stand out vividly. The first is that the needs and capacities of Canada and Japan complement one another to an extraordinary degree. The potential for further Japanese business involvement in Canada—to the mutual advantage of *both* sides—is enormous. The second conclusion is that if the full potential of this possible advantage is to be realized, a change of attitude—or at least a new awareness—is called for from both sides.

It is important, first, that Canadians learn to differentiate among the various origins and motives of foreign business involvement, recognizing that the consequences of Japanese business in Canada are mostly benign. It is imperative, also, that Japanese managers and public officials become more sensitive to Canadian desires for greater value added to resources before they are exported, and for moderation in the import of Japanese manufactures which compete with and displace Canadian-made products at home. Without these changes in perceptions and attitudes, the full symbiotic benefit of Japanese business involvement is likely to remain unrealized. As interaction and awareness grow between Canada and Japan, we may hope that this elusive alliance will mature to reach its full potential for a mutually rewarding, non-threatening relationship.

Abrégé

Les Canadiens, depuis longtemps habitués à la présence d'entreprises américaines dans leur pays, ont pris davantage conscience, ces dernières années, de la présence de plus en plus marquée d'un nouveau partenaire commercial : le Japon. La présente étude, fruit de plus de dix-huit mois de recherches par l'auteur, tant au Canada qu'au Japon, prouve la réalité de la place et des répercussions des investissements japonais au Canada.

La présence des Japonais place de nombreux Canadiens devant un dilemme d'importance. D'une part, cette infusion de capitaux, de compétences, de produits et de marchés d'achat japonais permet d'entrevoir d'importants bénéfices éventuels. D'autre part, les Canadiens qui constatent l'exportation de matières premières canadiennes vers le Japon et l'importation de produits manufacturés japonais au Canada se demandent, non sans raison, quels avantages ces échanges procurent au Canada. Plus fondamentalement encore, les Canadiens devenus circonspects se demandent si la croissance de la présence commerciale japonaise au Canada ne résultera pas, à la longue, en simple remplacement d'un maître étranger par un nouveau. On dispose de très peu d'indications précises permettant de se prononcer intelligemment sur l'importance de l'entreprise japonaise au Canada.

Le commerce canado-japonais : un aperçu

Le commerce entre le Canada et le Japon s'est accru radicalement depuis quelques années, à la fois en termes de valeur et en termes d'importance pour les deux pays. En 1982, le volume des échanges entre le Canada et le Japon s'élevait à plus de 8 milliards de dollars. A première vue, la relation commerciale semble satisfaisante pour les

Canadiens : la balance reste constamment en notre faveur. Les Canadiens ont toutefois raison de s'interroger à la fois sur l'évolution à court terme et sur les caractéristiques structurelles sous-jacentes. L'ampleur du surplus canadien en matière d'échanges bilatéraux a faibli substantiellement depuis 1979, tant en raison du ralentissement de la demande japonaise de matières premières canadiennes, qu'en raison d'une augmentation dramatique de l'importation d'automobiles japonaises directement en concurrence avec une industrie automobile nationale languissante.

Cette crise immédiate n'est qu'une des manifestations d'un déséquilibre qualitatif plus fondamental dans les échanges entre les deux pays. Le Canada exporte surtout des matières premières et des produits de base vers le Japon, alors que ses importations se composent presque exclusivement de produits manufacturés. Ce déséquilibre commercial qualitatif place le Canada dans une situation de pays moins développé par rapport au Japon, une situation qui semble s'aggraver plutôt que de s'améliorer. La méfiance et l'acrimonie ne peuvent qu'augmenter à moins que les Japonais ne prennent des mesures concrètes pour augmenter la transformation des matières premières avant leur exportation, pour faire fabriquer davantage de pièces détachées et d'autres composants au Canada et pour imposer un contrôle plus serré des exportations, vers le Canada, de produits manufacturés japonais menaçant la survie d'industries canadiennes. Les Japonais pourraient prendre ces quelques mesures sans qu'ils leur en coûte beaucoup.

Si on le situe dans le contexte de la croissance des échanges et de la taille des économies intérieures de chacun des pays, l'investissement direct privé entre le Canada et le Japon n'est pas très élevé. Les investissements japonais au Canada augmentent rapidement et dépassent maintenant le milliard de dollars, chiffre qui ne représente toutefois que moins de 1 pour cent du total des investissements étrangers au Canada.

A la différence des autres investisseurs, qui cherchent habituellement à diriger des compagnies affiliées au Canada, les investisseurs japonais cherchent avant tout d'assurer à leur pays un approvisionnement stable matières premières et à faciliter l'exportation de produits manufacturés au Japon. Ce qui confère des caractéristiques uniques à l'investissement japonais au Canada : il est surtout orienté vers les ressources naturelles et le marchandisage plutôt que vers la fabrication; il privilégie les prêts à long terme et la participation minoritaire plutôt que les prises de contrôle et il s'installe de préférence dans l'Ouest canadien plutôt que dans le centre industriel du pays. De par leur volonté d'offrir du financement et d'assurer des marchés ouverts sans chercher à prendre le contrôle, les objectifs japonais semblent compatibles avec les objectifs énoncés par le Canada de bien accueillir la participation étrangère qui ne menace pas notre souveraineté économique nationale. Le problème reste, toutefois, qu'une très faible portion des investissements japonais touche les activités de fabrication ou de transformation qui maximiserait au pays la création d'emplois et la valeur ajoutée. De l'avis de nombreux Canadiens, il est temps que les Japonais acceptent d'effectuer la transformation et la fabrication sur les lieux où ils obtiennent leurs matières premières, au lieu d'acheminer tout simplement l'énergie et les ressources vers l'industrie japonaise.

L'entreprise japonaise au Canada

Les sociétés japonaises entrent au Canada pour une variété de raisons et leur participation revêt plusieurs aspects. La présente étude en établit cinq catégories afin de permettre le classement et la discussion de leurs activités :
• l'énergie et les ressources,
• le marchandisage,
• le commerce,
• la fabrication,
• les services.

On a analysé les répercussions sur l'économie canadienne de toutes les entreprises canadiennes connues avec un actif d'au moins 10 000 $, ou des ventes annuelles d'au moins 5 000 $, et une participation japonaise majoritaire. On a aussi étudié la plupart des entreprises de cette catégorie avec une participation japonaise de 20 à 49 pour cent. Les 160 entreprises qui se rangent dans ces catégories employaient directement 13 419 personnes au Canada, à la fin de 1981. Le plus grand nombre d'employés se trouvaient dans la catégorie fabrication (4 667), suivis de près par le marchandisage (4 029) et les ressources (3 390). Si l'on range les 2 841 employés du secteur forestier et les 155 employés affectés à la production d'huile de colza dans le secteur des ressources plutôt que dans le secteur de la fabrication, ce secteur des ressources devient de loin le plus important groupe avec 6 386 employés ou 47,6 pour cent du total. La fabrication se range alors loin derrière, en troisième place, avec 1 671 employés ou 12,5 pour cent du total.

Au plan géographique, c'est en Colombie-Britannique qu'on retrouve, et de loin, le plus grand nombre d'emplois directs dans des entreprises à participation japonaise importante. Ces entreprises emploient 5 960 personnes ou 44,4 pour cent du total national. Bien que la plupart des emplois de la Colombie-Britannique se rangent dans le secteur des ressources, on trouve quand même un nombre important d'emplois dans le marchandisage, le commerce et la fabrication (dans la mesure où l'on range les produits forestiers sous la rubrique fabrication). C'est l'Ontario, où sont situées la plupart des sociétés de marchandisage et des banques, qui occupe le deuxième rang à titre d'employeur, avec 4 247 emplois. Au Québec, les 1 174 emplois sont répartis entre le marchandisage, le commerce et la fabrication. Ce sont les compagnies forestières (pâtes et papiers) du Nouveau-Brunswick qui assurent la plupart des 2 230 emplois des Maritimes. En Alberta, les entreprises japonaises emploient environ 400 personnes, surtout à l'élevage du bétail et à la culture du colza; on en trouve le même nombre au Manitoba, presque toutes dans le secteur du marchandisage. Les emplois directs qui relèvent des Japonais sont presque inexistants à Terre-Neuve, en Nouvelle-Écosse, à l'Î'le du-Prince-Édouard, en Saskatchewan et dans les Territoires.

Les chiffres sur l'emploi direct ont été soit puisés dans diverses publications, sait recueillis en cours d'entrevues. Les estimations de traitements et salaires ainsi que de la valeur ajoutée directs ont été compilés d'après des tableaux d'entrées-sorties de Statistique Canada, en s'appuyant sur le rapport canadien moyen salaires et production, par employé, dans chacune des activités énoncées.

Selon ces estimations, les sociétés japonaises ont versé 225,7 millions de dollars en salaires et traitements bruts au Canada en 1981; 44 pour cent de cette somme ont été versés dans le secteur manufacturier, y compris la fabrication de produits forestiers. Le total de la valeur ajoutée directe par les mêmes compagnies était de 387,6 millions de dollars principalement dans les secteurs des ressources, qui représentaient 43 pour cent du total, et celui de la fabrication, qui représentait 34 pour cent du total.

Les répercussions économiques

Les chiffres sus-mentionnés représentent les effets mesurables *directs* des sociétés japonaises au Canada. Ces effets directs ont, par ailleurs, un effet d'entraînement sur la production de biens et services dans la mesure où les employés et les fournisseurs des entreprises japonaises dépensent les revenus qu'ils ont reçus. C'est ainsi que la demande initiale directe créée par les sociétés japonaises suscite une production et une valeur ajoutée supplémentaires indirectes dans les autres secteurs de l'économie. Il faut donc songer à une combinaison d'effets directs et d'effets induits si l'on parle de l'ensemble des répercussions économiques de ces sociétés.

En s'appuyant sur les profils de la demande directe et sur la nature des activités en cause, on a utilisé les modèles d'entrées-sorties de Statistique Canada pour simuler les répercussions économiques des entreprises japonaises au Canada. On a pu ainsi obtenir une estimation à la fois du total des emplois créés dans chacun des groupes et de la valeur ajoutée, répartis entre quarante secteurs économiques, ainsi que de la distribution de l'emploi et de la valeur ajoutée dans chacune des provinces.

La simulation a permis de constater que de 36 000 à 40 000 emplois découlent des activités d'entreprises japonaises au Canada, ce qui ajoute environ 1,2 milliards de dollars au produit intérieur brut (PIB). Ces chiffres peuvent paraître limités si on les compare à ceux de l'ensemble de l'économie. Le total des emplois reliés aux entreprises japonaises, par exemple, touche moins de 1 pour cent de la population active canadienne. Les effets sont cependant significatifs. Dans l'actuel climat de récession, alors que les gouvernements du Canada affectent des sommes énormes aux tentatives de création d'emplois et de stimulation de la production intérieure, les sociétés japonaises génèrent des milliers d'emplois et plus d'un milliard de dollars de production intérieure à coût presque nul pour les contribuables. Ce qui ne veut pas dire cependant que nous ne payons rien pour ces avantages : il faut évidemment tenir compte des sorties de ressources naturelles et de dividendes ainsi que d'une certaine perte de maîtrise de notre économie intérieure. Il reste cependant qu'en raison de la nature de l'investissement japonais, les coûts financiers et la perte de maîtrise sont très minimes.

La répartition géographique des avantages générés par l'activité des entreprises japonaises est aussi fort significative. Comme prévu, la simulation indique que c'est dans l'Ouest, et surtout en Colombie-Britannique, où 60 pour cent du total national sont générés que l'on trouve la valeur ajoutée la plus élevée. D'autre part, les avantages de l'emploi sont répartis beaucoup plus uniformément : 53 pour cent des emplois dans l'Est du Canada, surtout en Ontario et au Québec, et 47 pour cent dans les provinces des Prairies et de l'Ouest, surtout en Colombie-Britannique. Alors que les répercussions immédiates des activités commerciales japonaises au Canada semblent être fortement concentrées, les bénéfices dérivés sont répartis beaucoup plus uniformément dans le pays. La vaste diffusion des bénéfices révélés dans cette analyse constitue un trait fort significatif de la présence commerciale japonaise que les Canadiens, qui ont tendance à s'arrêter surtout aux effets immédiats plus évidents (et fortement concentrés), ne reconnaissent pas toujours.

Les effet intangibles

La présence commerciale japonaise exerce d'autres influences profondes qui sont plus difficiles à quantifier. L'étude porte tour à tour sur le rôle des sociétés commerciales japonaises et la fonction des banques, ainsi que sur le financement des projets, des marchés d'achat et des transferts de technologie et de gestion.

Les sociétés commerciales

La pleine importance économique des sociétés commerciales japonaises dépasse de beaucoup leurs répercussions sur l'emploi direct et la consommation de biens et services. Fortes de leurs énormes ressources financières et de leurs vastes réseaux mondiaux d'information et de communications, ces sociétés jouent un rôle décisif dans la stimulation du commerce et des investissements au Canada. L'exportation vers le Japon, en particulier de matières premières, représente environ 65 pour cent des activités des sociétés commerciales. Les importations en provenance du Japon représentent environ 26 pour cent, tandis que le commerce entre le Canada et les autres pays se partage les autres 9 pour cent. Les 9 sociétés commerciales générales agissant au Canada ont eu un chiffre total d'affaires de près de 5 milliards de dollars dans ce pays en 1980, traitant 71 pour cent de toutes les exportations canadiennes vers le Japon et 41 pour cent des importations canadiennes en provenance du Japon. Outre leurs activités bilatérales, les sociétés commerciales ont exporté pour 256 millions de dollars vers des pays tiers et importé au Canada des produits d'une valeur de 156 millions de dollars.

En 1981, ces mêmes sociétés avaient investi l'équivalent de 169 millions de dollars US au Canada, ce qui représentait 20 pour cent de tous les investissements japonais au Canada. Plus important encore, elles avaient, grâce à des coentreprises, agi comme promoteurs et catalyseurs pour attirer au Canada, les investissements de d'autres sociétés japonaises. Leurs répercussions se font donc sentir bien au-delà de leurs simples activités d'investissement immédiates.

Les banques

En dépit de pouvoir exercer directement des activités bancaires commerciales au Canada, douze banques japonaises ont ouvert au pays des bureaux offrant une variété de services. De plus, les révisions apportées à la Loi canadienne sur les banques, entrées en vigueur en janvier 1981, ont permis une participation plus directe et plus substantielle, principalement en matière de financement des grands projets de mise en valeur et d'autres services commerciaux de gros.

Le financement des projets

Bien que leur incidence directe sur le secteur des ressources canadiennes sait minime, les Japonais jouent un rôle indirect décisif en proposant les prêts et les marchés d'achat nécessaires à la viabilité de certains des mégaprojets les plus ambitieux du Canada. Malgré l'impossibilité de mesurer précisément le plein impact d'une telle participation indirecte, elle représente probablement, pour les Canadiens, l'avantage le plus substantiel et le plus marqué de la présence commerciale japonaise.

La politique énergétique nationale du Canada décourage la participation directe des entreprises japonaises aux grands projets pétroliers et à l'exportation de pétrole ou de gaz canadiens, jusqu'à ce que le Canada atteigne l'autosuffisance énergétique. Les Japonais ont néanmoins intérêt à aider les Canadiens à explorer et à mettre en valeur d'éventuelles sources de pétrole et de gaz, car si la production du Canada dépasse ses besoins intérieurs, les Canadiens et les Japonais pourront profiter de l'exportation des surplus vers le Japon. Même si on ne permet pas l'exportation de pétrole, les nouvelles découvertes tendent à réduire la pression sur le marché mondial, ce qui profite au Japon. Compte tenu de cette situation, les Japonais affectent des sommes importantes au financement par des prêts de travaux pétroliers canadiens dans l'Arctique et dans les sables bitumineux de l'Alberta, et ce, a des taux d'intérêt souvent extrêmement favorables et sans garantie de remboursement. En agissant ainsi, sans aucune assurance du succès des projets ou de l'approbation des exportations de pétrole par le gouvernement, s'il y a réussite, les Japonais assument aussi leur part entière de risque.

Les marchés d'achat

On ne peut investir les importantes sommes nécessaires à la mise en valeur de nombreuses ressources naturelles du Canada, en particulier du charbon, sans obtenir de fermes garanties d'une demande soutenue. Bien qu'il existe une faible demande de charbon canadien dans certains petits pays d'Asie et d'Amérique latine, le plus gros client éventuel reste, certes, le Japon.

Les sociétés japonaises détiennent une participation minoritaire dans plusieurs mines de charbon, surtout dans le sud de la Colombie-Britannique; elles ont aussi prêté des fonds à d'autres mines. Les entreprises japonaises ont toutefois passé des contrats d'achat, souvent d'une durée de quinze ans, avec toutes les entreprises auxquelles elles participent, en vue de la vente de la production à ces entreprises japonaises. Ce sont ces marchés d'achat, plus que le financement direct, qui assurent la viabilité des mines.

La technologie et la gestion

La recherche insinue qu'exception faite d'une poignée d'exemples, le Canada a très peu reçu à ce jour en matière de transfert de technologie du Japon. Ce qui ne devrait probablement pas étonner dans la mesure où les Japonais s'intéressent surtout à l'extraction et à la transformation des resources naturelles, activités dans lesquelles ils n'ont que très peu d'expérience directe. Il est probable que la participation technologique japonaise deviendra plus importante dans certains projets de mise en valeur de ressources à forte incidence technologique tels que la production de gaz naturel liquéfié et la construction de complexes pétrochimiques prévus pour l'avenir.

En règle générale, la présence commerciale japonaise au Canada semble n'avoir exercé qu'une influence négligeable sur les pratiques de gestion. La gestion de la plupart des filiales japonaises au Canada s'apparente à celle des entreprises canadiennes comparables. Cela s'explique, en partie, par le fait que les pratiques de gestion japonaises s'appliquent avant tout aux activités de fabrication : or les Japonais ne s'adonnent à peu près pas à de telles activités au Canada. Les gestionnaires japonais interviewés, dans le cadre de cette recherche, ont mentionné l'influence des syndicats canadiens comme un obstacle majeur à toute tentative de transférer des méthodes de gestion. Les pratiques de gestion japonaises classiques, fondées sur une communication ouverte et directe entre la direction et les travailleurs ainsi que sur des valeurs communes, pourraient s'avérer inopérables au Canada compte tenu du militantisme et de la rigidité perçue des syndicats canadiens.

L'intangible alliance : une conclusion personnelle

L'auteur du présent rapport a discuté pendant 18 mois avec des centaines de particuliers, tant japonais que canadiens. Deux conclusions s'imposent. La première est que les besoins et les aptitudes du Canada et du Japon se complètent de façon extraordinaire. Les perspectives d'une participation plus poussée de l'entreprise japonaise au Canada—au profit des deux parties—sont énormes. La seconde est que dans le but de tirer pleinement parti de cet éventuel avantage, il faudra que les deux parties effectuent un changement d'attitude ou, à tout le moins, s'ouvrent à une nouvelle prise de conscience.

Il est d'abord très important que les Canadiens apprennent à différencier les diverses origines et motivations des gens d'affaires étrangers et à reconnaitre que les conséquences de la participation japonaise au Canada sont plutôt favorables. Il est aussi essentiel que les gestionnaires et fonctionnaires japonais se sensibilisent davantage au désir des Canadiens de bénéficier, a la fois, d'une plus grande valeur de leurs ressources avant l'exportation et d'un ralentissement de l'importation des manufactures japonaises en concurrence et même en remplacement des produits fabriqués au Canada. Sans ces changements de perception et d'attitudes, on ne pourra que difficilement profiter des avantages symbiotiques de la participation commerciale japonaise. À mesure que croîtront cette interaction et cette prise de conscience entre le Canada et le Japon, nous pouvons espérer que cette intangible alliance mûrira de manière à réaliser toutes les possibilités d'une relation enrichissante et sécurisante.

List of Tables

List of Figures

1: Introduction

Canadians have long been accustomed to the presence of foreign business in Canada: the extent of foreign control of Canada's economy is greater than that of any other major country in the world. But 'foreign' business, for most Canadians, means American business, as United States (US)-owned subsidiaries have traditionally dominated both Canada's international trade and its domestic economy.

In recent years, however, a striking new phenomenon has arisen: the growing presence of Japanese firms in Canada. Canadians view the Japanese presence with a mixture of welcome and apprehension. They see, on the one hand, an infusion of Japanese capital, skills, products and purchase contracts that may provide an important new stimulus to the balanced growth and development of the Canadian economy. At the same time, Canadians viewing the export of Canadian raw materials to Japan and the import of Japanese manufactured products to Canada, ask—rightly—just what benefits all of this activity brings to Canada. Even more basically, wary Canadians question whether the growing Japanese business presence will, in the long run, merely substitute a new foreign master for a traditional one.

For several reasons, Canadians seem to be more apprehensive about economic and business relations with Japan than with other countries. The most fundamental reason is that Canadians simply do not *know* the Japanese. Japan is a very distant land with a unique culture. Canadians may not like all aspects of American and Western European businesses in Canada, but at least, in these instances, they are dealing with people they know. Secondly, the Japanese have a reputation among many Canadians for being highly aggressive and sometimes ruthless in their business dealings

1

with foreigners. Rightly or wrongly, a fear exists that in any extensive dealings with Japanese, Canadians will be 'taken to the cleaners.' Thirdly, latent memories of the Second World War unquestionably fuel suspicion and fear of Japan in some Canadians.

Some positive steps have been taken to facilitate the flow of communication and understanding between the two countries. A variety of cultural exchange programs have been developed, and several Canadian universities have instituted studies of Japan and the Japanese business system. Each year the Canada-Japan Businessmen's Conference, initiated in 1978, brings together senior business executives of both countries for a candid exchange of views. A high-level Survey Mission on Overseas Investment Environment, sent to Canada by Japan's Ministry of International Trade and Industry in April 1982, helped to clarify the concerns of both Japanese and Canadians, as did the trade discussions held between Prime Ministers Trudeau and Nakasone in Tokyo on 17-18 January 1983.[1] A major task-force study has recommended that over the next three years, the Canadian government put $20 million into an Asia-Pacific Foundation devoted to the study of cultural, economic and other public-affairs issues related to Japan and the Pacific.[2]

Despite these steps, misunderstanding and suspicion remain. The Japanese are still indignant at what they consider to have been unfair action by Canada Customs in impeding Canadian import of Japanese autos in 1982. At the same time, Canadian newspapers and public officials condemn with growing vehemence what they see as a deliberate failure by Japanese companies to process Canadian raw materials in Canada, to obtain manufactures from Canadian suppliers, and to increase investment in Canadian manufacturing.

Canadians have woefully little evidence on which to base intelligent judgements about the role of Japanese business in Canada. Traditional studies of foreign ownership in Canada[3] are necessarily overwhelmed by US-controlled firms whose motives and forms of involvement in Canada differ strikingly from those of the Japanese. Several recent studies in the United States focus specifically on Japanese business in that country.[4] But Japan's business involvement in Canada differs substantially from that in the United States, so that US-based studies have only marginal relevance to Canada.

This report provides a timely and comprehensive profile of the function and impact of Japanese business activity in Canada. It is based on eighteen months of research in Canada and Japan, including both widespread examination of public documents and files, and in-depth personal interviews with executives of some fifty Japanese companies and with other officials.

Chapter 2 of the report presents an overview of the evolution and nature of trade and investment relationships between Canada and Japan. The discussion also compares Japanese and American business activity in Canada, emphasizing differences in their control objectives and the effects of their trade generation. The three chapters which follow present a detailed analysis of the function and impact of Japan's involvement. Chapter 3 describes the magnitude and nature of Japanese businesses and examines their direct economic effects in five economic sectors. Chapter 4 traces the induced effects on the Canadian economy of the purchases of goods and services by Japanese companies, by economic sector and by province. Chapter 5 examines important non-quantifiable effects of Japanese trading companies, banks, resource-development loans, and long-term purchase contracts. A final chapter looks to the future by identifying areas of further Japanese involvement, as well as perceived obstacles to the development of a fully satisfactory trade relationship.

Notes

1. *Globe and Mail* (Toronto), various articles, 17, 18, 19 January 1983.

2. John Bruk, *Asia Pacific Foundation.*

3. See, for example, A.E. Safarian, *The Performance of Foreign Owned Firms in Canada;* I.A. Litvak, *et al., Dual Loyalty: Canadian-US Business Arrangements;* Alan M. Rugman, *Multinationals in Canada: Theory, Performance, and Economic Impact.*

4. Conservation of Human Resource Project, *Economic Impact of the Japanese Business Community in the United States;* and Susan Knight, *Japan's Expanding Manufacturing Presence in the United States: A Profile.*

2: Canadian Japanese Business: An Overview

This chapter presents an overview of business activity between Canada and Japan, highlighting features of particular relevance to a discussion of Japanese business in Canada. It focuses first on bilateral trade relations, then on patterns of investment flows.

Trade Patterns

Trade activity between Canada and Japan has grown substantially in recent years. (See Figure 2-1.) Except for slight declines in 1975 and 1982, the volume of trade has grown every year of the last twenty, with growth rates often exceeding 20 per cent per year. Total bilateral trade between the two countries reached a high of $8.5 billion in 1981. Volumes and growth rates of imports, exports and total bilateral trade are detailed in Table 2-1, below. These rates appear much less dramatic, of course, if the effects of price inflation are eliminated. While Canada-Japan trade grew at an average rate of 16 per cent per annum from 1971 to 1982, the growth rates adjusted for changes in the Wholesale Price Index averaged only 6.4 per cent for the same period.

As the volume of trade has increased, so has its importance to both Japan and Canada. In 1973 Japan replaced Britain as the second-most-important market for Canadian exports, after the United States (USA), and it remains so today. For Canadians, Japan offers not only the fastest growing potential export market, but also the most promising and viable alternative to dependence on the USA. For Japan, also, trade with Canada has assumed vital importance. Canada is the

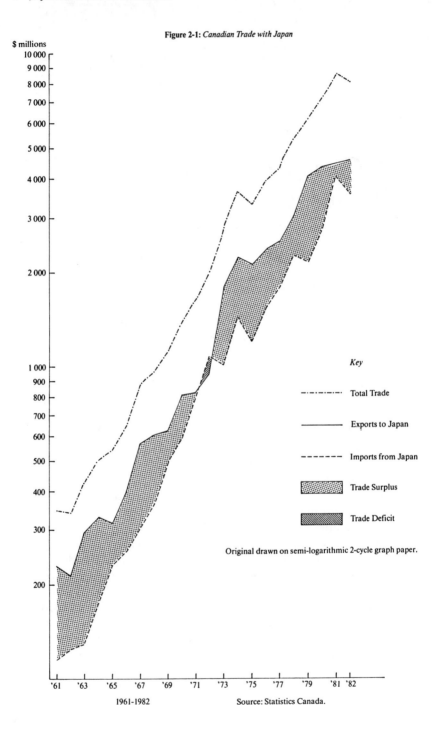

Figure 2-1: *Canadian Trade with Japan*

$ millions

Key

- - · - · - · -   Total Trade

─────────   Exports to Japan

- - - - - - -   Imports from Japan

▨   Trade Surplus

▨   Trade Deficit

Original drawn on semi-logarithmic 2-cycle graph paper.

1961-1982   Source: Statistics Canada.

Table 2-1: *Canadian Trade with Japan*

Year	Exports $ million	Exports Rate of Growth	Imports $ million	Imports Rate of Growth	Total Trade^b $ million	Total Trade^b Rate of Growth	Trade Surplus $ million	Trade Surplus Rate of Growth	Trade Surplus as a Fraction of Total Trade
1983	4728	3%	4409	25%	9137	13%	319	-69%	0.03
1982	4571	2%	3527	-13%	8090	-5%	1040	133%	0.13
1981	4497	3%	4039	44%	8526	19%	458	-72%	0.05
1980	4357	7%	2792	30%	7166	15%	1575	-18%	0.22
1979	4077	34%	2157	-5%	6234	17%	1920	147%	0.31
1978	3053	21%	2276	26%	5329	23%	777	9%	0.15
1977	2513	5%	1803	18%	4316	10%	710	-18%	0.16
1976	2392	13%	1524	26%	3916	18%	868	-5%	0.18
1975	2117	-5%	1205	-16%	3323	-9%	912	14%	0.27
1974	2227	23%	1430	40%	3657	30%	798	2%	0.22
1973	1804	88%	1018	-5%	2821	39%	786	—	0.28
1972	961	16%	1072	34%	2033	25%	-110	—	—
1971	829	2%	802	38%	1631	17%	27	-88%	0.02
1970	810	30%	582	17%	1392	24%	228	77%	0.16
1969	625	3%	496	38%	1121	16%	129	-48%	0.12
1968	607	6%	360	18%	967	10%	246	-8%	0.25
1967	572	45%	305	21%	877	36%	267	89%	0.30
1966	394	25%	253	10%	647	18%	141	64%	0.22
1965	316	-4%	230	32%	546	8%	86	-45%	0.16
1964	330	11%	174	34%	504	18%	156	-6%	0.31
1963	296	38%	130	4%	426	26%	166	87%	0.39
1962	214	-8%	125	8%	339	-2%	89	-23%	0.26
1961	231		116		347		115		0.33

Notes
a. Source: Statistics Canada.
b. Totals may not tally due to rounding.

third-most-important supplier to Japan, if petroleum imports are excluded. Japan relies on Canada for nearly 100 per cent of its imported rapeseed oil, two-thirds of its lead ore, and almost half of its buckwheat, plywood, lumber and asbestos, as well as significant proportions of other minerals and grains.

Analysis of the trade flows reveals some important patterns which colour any discussion of Japanese business in Canada. The first of these patterns shows that the trade balance between the two countries is consistently in Canada's favour. In every year of the past two decades, with the sole exception of 1972, the overall value of Canadian exports to Japan has exceeded the value of imports. Canada's trade surplus with Japan peaked at nearly $2 billion in 1979 and stands among the largest which Canada has ever realized with any country. The Japanese repeatedly cite this chronic surplus as proof that the bilateral trade relationship is skewed highly in Canada's favour.

Canadians, on the other hand, view the relationship with growing apprehension. They note that while the overall balance remains in Canada's favour, the surplus has shrunk dramatically in recent years, from $1.9 billion in 1979 to only $0.5 billion in 1981, or from 31 per cent of the overall trade volume to only 5 per cent; it has, however, partially rebounded in 1982 and 1983. Analysis of trade flows by product (as shown in Tables 2-2 and 2-3) shows that this deterioration was caused mainly by a slow-down in the growth of demand for exports to Japan of Canadian raw materials and by a substantial increase in Canadian imports of Japanese automobiles. The latter phenomenon has produced a ground-swell of demands for import restrictions in Canada or for local-content requirements for manufactured products if the Japanese fail to restrain their auto exports voluntarily. The auto dispute has been cooled for the time being by the negotiation of temporary quotas by the Canadian and Japanese governments. Under the first such agreement, struck in 1982, Japanese auto imports were limited to 153 000 units, which represented a reduction of 25 per cent from the previous year.[1] A renewed agreement announced in August 1983 limits Japanese imports to 202 600 units for the fifteen-month period between 1 January 1983 and 31 March 1984. The new limit is designed to reduce the market share of Japanese cars from 25 per cent to 20 per cent.[2] Japanese officials have stated, however, that they will not agree to an extension of restrictions beyond March 1984, and Canada's case for further limits is likely to weaken with renewed growth of the Canadian economy.

Table 2-2: *Major Canadian Exports to Japan ($ 000)[a]*

	1980	1981	1982	Jan.-June 1983
Coal	588 989	680 758	837 041	415 903
Rapeseed	317 940	389 355	382 799	189 579
Lumber	501 355	367 223	354 493	193 111
Wheat	303 110	368 416	299 694	159 412
Wood pulp	456 934	388 454	268 526	162 860
Copper	354 679	304 004	236 365	113 887
Aluminum including alloys	205 251	209 247	209 180	*[b]
Pork (fresh or frozen)	114 989	156 263	181 976	107 541
Barley	97 397	191 577	136 066	74 818
Roe (salmon, herring and other fish)	*	88 003	86 350	85 107
Potash (potassium chloride, muriate)	61 816	61 570	70 337	39 251
Iron ore concentrated	81 154	82 235	69 285	29 625
Propane liquified	50 101	61 106	69 094	38 285
Alcohols & derivatives	28 526	80 570	62 563	75 520
Molybdenum in ores concentrate & scrap	113 468	60 247	53 492	8 333
Silver (ores and concentrates)	63 479	67 570	48 672	30 365
Logs	44 143	35 992	48 152	38 609
Pulpwood chips	43 326	43 477	41 009	15 451
Flaxseed	35 504	37 773	33 944	16 156
Zinc	34 161	51 702	32 352	15 257
Gold (ore and concentrates)	65 673	44 453	31 085	20 526
Squid and shellfish NES	*	15 171	29 782	11 818
Alfalfa (dehydrated)	23 883	20 998	28 567	18 048
Chemical elements NES	26 244	7 985	21 533	9 617
Earth drilling & related Mach. & parts NES	*	985	20 189	67 124
Radioactive elements & isotopes	*	1 577	19 617	7 844
Tallow	18 481	18 401	19 418	5 833
Liner board	16 860	18 414	17 654	6 014
Card-punch sort-tab computers & parts	19 307	18 989	16 991	7 748
Ham (not cured or cooked)	9 999	22 595	16 696	2 979
Ferrosilicon	15 697	18 595	15 268	4 820
Wrap paper	15 768	6 408	14 592	7 730
Hydrocarbons and derivatives	22 114	13 587	13 738	5 174
Metal bearing (ores and concentrates)	11 247	6 521	13 276	1 723
Pelleted screenings (animal feed)	19 777	13 310	12 559	6 344
Beef, frozen, boneless	10 642	12 662	11 368	3 931
Horse meat (fresh or frozen)	*	11 107	10 954	4 513
Lead (ores and concentrates)	68 605	25 005	10 642	nil
Plastic & synthetic rubber (unshaped) NES	*	11 289	8 724	4 842
Salmon	*	26 580	4 200	2 702
Crude petroleum	nil	nil	nil	13 767
Malt	*	*	*	29 404
Subtotal	3 831 619	4 040 174	3 858 243	2 051 571
Miscellaneous	524 899	457 486	712 985	285 026
Total	4 356 518	4 497 660	4 571 228	2 336 597

Notes
a. Source: Statistics Canada.
b. *indicates that figures are not available because of revised classification groupings.

Table 2-3: *Major Canadian Imports from Japan ($ 000)[a]*

	1980	1981	1982	Jan.-June 1983
Cars, new	568 253	991 882	745 291	397 670
Motor vehicles, other	136 338	217 602	337 685	243 268
Tape players, recorders and tape	*[b]	180 044	232 024	153 332
Televisions, radios, phonographs	127 209	202 586	173 882	98 205
Photographic goods	*	188 722	123 253	73 070
Electric equipment components	*	166 093	117 288	62 090
Motor vehicle parts, except engines	41 472	88 585	111 433	66 152
Station wagons, new	38 087	54 853	77 429	54 824
Pipes and tubes, iron and steel	*	86 510	71 029	19 085
Tires and tubes	73 272	73 288	53 189	29 701
Photocopy and similar machines & parts	*	78 243	52 588	29 044
Electric generating equipment	136 670	36 520	52 142	24 459
Plate, sheet and strip steel	70 030	98 206	49 034	17 254
Kitchen utensils, cutlery and tableware	33 915	40 800	47 824	17 450
Electronic computers & parts	17 230	24 610	44 494	47 556
Polyester broad-woven fabrics and parts	13 606	34 106	40 196	19 322
Watches, clocks, jewellery, silverware	34 889	55 522	39 131	14 039
Well casing, new	62 480	68 293	36 780	9 749
Microwave ovens	17 892	40 463	31 012	17 757
Unexposed photofilm and plates	21 057	26 673	30 717	15 155
Alumina	*	41 548	28 038	27 518
Basic hardware, nails, fasteners, etc.	25 840	28 413	24 962	14 661
Bicycles and parts	26 734	26 668	23 303	24 051
Fish, fish & marine-animal oil	27 076	24 544	22 879	11 715
Calculating machines & parts	35 651	20 350	22 379	13 406
Petrol/coal products, machinery & parts	*	1 445	19 374	11 110
Bars and rods, steel	25 325	29 997	19 876	11 411
Track-laying tractors and used tractors	17 351	16 333	18 266	6 988
Iron and steel pipe fittings	*	20 770	17 500	7 297
Organic chemicals	21 437	21 910	16 732	9 902
Oranges, mandarins, tangerines (fresh)	13 808	13 780	15 643	nil
Power-driven hand tools	*	16 909	14 113	7 682
Broad-woven fabrics, mixed fibres	*	13 966	14 089	7 652
Excavator-type, crane, shovel (power)	21 200	16 214	13 875	1 898
Telecommunications & related equipment	117 865	12 741	10 479	10 740
Heat exchangers, industrial and parts	*	5 381	3 955	23 843

Table 2-3 continued

	1980	1981	1982	Jan.-June 1983
Lathes, metal-working, automatic	11 246	9 650	2 284	1 225
Ships and boats	*	23 702	nil	10 706
Subtotal	1 735 933	3 097 922	2 754 168	1 611 078
Miscellaneous	1 056 227	941 145	772 951	365 503
Total	2 792 160	4 039 067	3 527 119	1 976 581

Notes
a. Source: Statistics Canada.
b. *indicates that figures for 1980 are not available because of revised classification groupings.

Canadians are also disturbed by the sectoral distribution of their trade with Japan: Canada's exports to Japan are mainly raw or semi-processed materials, while nearly all of the imports from Japan are fully manufactured products. The exact proportion of manufactured goods in Canada's exports to Japan varies, depending on whose figures are used. According to Statistics Canada, manufactured goods account for less than 3 per cent of the total. On the other hand, the *White Papers on Trade,* published by Japan's Ministry of International Trade and Industry (MITI), indicate that manufactured exports have increased steadily to some 16 per cent of overall Canadian exports to Japan. The discrepancy comes from the fact that the Japanese figures include semi-manufactured goods such as aluminum ingots, while Canadian statistics calculate only fully-

Table 2-4: *Canadian Manufactured Exports to Japan[a]*

	1977	1978	1979	1980
Canadian Statistics[b]				
Total exports (to Japan)	2 513	2 035	4 083	4 364
Manufactured goods exports	50	64	93	106
% of total exports	2.0	2.1	2.3	2.4
Japanese Statistics[c]				
Total imports (from Canada)	2 881	3 191	4 105	4 724
Manufactured goods imports	249	410	456	758
% of total imports	8.6	12.8	11.1	16.0

Notes
a. Source: *White Papers on Trade,* Ministry of International Trade & Industry, Japan; and Statistics Canada.
b. In millions of Canadian dollars.
c. In millions of US dollars.

manufactured goods. These differences, which dramatize a lack of communication between the two countries, are illustrated in Table 2-4.

Table 2-5 further analyses the composition of trade by degree of processing or manufacturing. Although the proportion of manufactured goods in Canadian exports to Japan has increased slightly in recent years, nearly 75 per cent of 1981 exports consisted of crude or fabricated materials, while 81 per cent of the imports from Japan were fully-manufactured end products. Moreover, the proportion of end products in Canada's imports from Japan has been growing steadily for two decades. Many Canadians think that this *qualitative* imbalance is far more significant than the overall value of the goods traded, since it relegates Canada to the equivalent of developing-country status in relation to Japan. Canadians use these observations to bolster their demands that Japanese companies perform additional processing of materials in Canada and import more Canadian-manufactured products in order to increase value added and employment in Canada.

A Comparison of Japanese and US Trade with Canada

Because of the dominance of United States (US) trade, it is instructive to compare patterns of Canadian-Japanese trade with those of Canadian-US trade. Table 2-6 presents aggregate data on Canada-USA trade. Although Canadian trade has grown both with the USA and with Japan, trade with Japan has tended, in recent years, to grow at a marginally faster rate: Canada's trade with Japan has grown at a rate of 16.0 per cent per annum since 1975, as compared with a growth rate of 13.0 per cent per annum for Canada's trade with the USA. Moreover, the continuous surplus position which Canada has enjoyed in trade with Japan is not present in Canadian-US trade, which tends to oscillate between surpluses and deficits.

Figures 2-2 and 2-3 contrast the manufactured composition of Canada's trade with Japan and the USA. While Canada shows a significant deficit in its trade of manufactures with both countries, the trade in manufactures with the USA is, in relative terms, more favourable to Canada than is that with Japan.

Some 34 per cent of 1981 exports to the USA were end products, and another 38 per cent were fabricated materials, in contrast to only 2 per cent and 31 per cent, respectively, of Canadian exports to Japan. On the import side, 67 per cent of Canada's imports from the USA were end products, in contrast to 81 per cent of Canadian imports from Japan.

Table 2-5: *Canadian Trade with Japan: Changes in Composition[a]*

	Exports					Imports				
	1965	1970	1975	1980	1981	1965	1970	1975	1980	1981
Food, feed, beverages and tobacco										
• $ millions	109.8	129.5	536.1	763.7	1 057.6	8.7	17.8	34.3	48.7	47.0
• % of total exports/imports	35%	16%	25%	17%	24%	4%	3%	3%	2%	1%
• Averge R.O.G.[b] over 16 years					15.2%					11.1%
Crude materials, inedible										
• $ millions	124.7	405.4	1 171.7	1 959.0	1 929.0	0.3	1.2	5.6	42.5	46.9
• % of total exports/imports	40%	50%	55%	45%	43%	0.00%	0.00%	0.00%	2%	1%
• Average R.O.G. over 16 years					18.7%					37.1%
Fabricated materials, inedible										
• $ millions	75.9	247.8	341.7	1 535.4	1 380.7	85.7	169.6	354.8	483.8	630.2
• % of total exports/imports	24%	31%	16%	35%	31%	37%	29%	29%	17%	16%
• Average R.O.G. over 16 years					19.9%					13.3%
Food products, inedible										
• $ millions	5.4	27.2	66.3	105.7	112.2	133.3	388.5	805.5	2 193.7	3 286.8
• % of total exports/imports	2%	3%	3%	3%	2%	58%	67%	67%	78%	81%
• Average R.O.G. over 16 years					20.9%					22.2%

Table 2-5 continued

	Exports					Imports				
	1965	1970	1975	1980	1981	1965	1970	1975	1980	1981
Other transactions										
• $ millions	0.4	0.8	1.6	6.6	5.6	2.1	4.7	5.1	23.4	28.1
• % of total exports/imports	0.00%	0.00%	0.00%	0.00%	0.00%	1%	1%	0.00%	1%	1%
• Average R.O.G. over 16 years					17.9%					17.6%
Totals[c]										
• $ millions	316.2	810.1	2 117.3	4 370.5	4 485.4	230.1	581.7	1 205.3	2 795.8	4 039.1
• % of total exports/imports	100%	100%	100%	100%	100%	100%	100%	100%	100%	100%
• Average R.O.G. over 16 years					18.0%					19.6%

Notes
a. Source: Statistics Canada.
b. R.O.G.: rate of growth.
c. Totals may not tally due to rounding.

Table 2-6: Canadian Trade with the USA[a]

Year	Exports $ million	Exports Rate of Growth	Imports $ million	Imports Rate of Growth	Total Trade[b] $ million	Total Trade Rate of Growth	Trade Surplus $ million	Trade Surplus Rate of Growth	Trade Surplus as a Fraction of Total Trade
1982	57 220	6%	48 194	-11%	105 414	-3%	9 026	—	9%
1981	53 800	15%	54 311	12%	108 211	14%	-411	—	—
1980	46 855	8%	48 414	7%	95 268	7%	-1 559	—	-2%
1979	43 463	19%	45 420	28%	88 883	23%	-1 956	—	-2%
1978	36 666	21%	35 436	20%	72 103	20%	1 230	79%	2%
1977	30 319	20%	29 630	15%	59 949	18%	688	—	1%
1976	25 233	20%	25 652	9%	50 985	14%	-519	—	-1%
1975	21 030	1%	23 559	10%	44 589	6%	-2 529	—	-6%
1974	20 763	25%	21 357	29%	42 119	27%	-594	—	-1%
1973	16 612	22%	16 497	28%	33 109	25%	115	-84%	0.3%
1972	13 575	16%	12 877	18%	26 452	17%	699	-4%	3%
1971	11 682	9%	10 951	10%	22 632	10%	731	-3%	3%
1970	10 670	4%	9 917	-3%	20 587	0%	753	2 410%	4%
1969	10 274	15%	10 243	13%	20 517	14%	30	—	0.1%
1968	8 923	26%	9 048	0%	17 971	11%	-126	—	-1%
1967	7 079	17%	9 056	27%	16 137	23%	-1 976	—	-12%
1966	6 028	25%	7 136	18%	13 164	21%	-1 108	—	-8%
1965	4 839	13%	6 045	17%	10 884	15%	-1 206	—	-11%
1964	4 271	13%	5 164	16%	9 435	15%	-893	—	-9%
1963	3 766	4%	4 444	3%	8 210	4%	-678	—	-8%
1962	3 608	16%	4 300	11%	7 908	13%	-692	—	-9%
1961	3 107	—	3 864	—	6 971	—	-757	—	-11%

Notes
a. Source: Statistics Canada.
b. Totals may not tally because of rounding.

Figure 2-2: *Canadian Exports to USA and Japan, 1981ª*

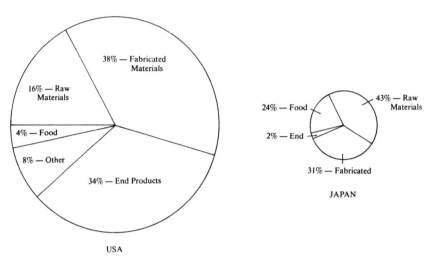

While the imbalance between primary exports and manufactured imports, as these pertain to Japan, seems high in relative terms, it is less significant in absolute terms. Table 2-7 isolates Canada's imbalance of trade in fabricated materials and end products, both with Japan and with the USA. If, as some Canadians argue, a Canadian deficit in the balance of manufactured and processed goods traded signifies an export of manufacturing employment and value added to the surplus country, then such losses to the USA are nearly ten times as large as those to Japan. This raises the interesting question of why Canadians seem to focus so much more intently on the small imbalance of manufactures traded with Japan than on the much larger potential employment loss through trade with the USA.

Figure 2-3: *Canadian Imports from USA and Japan, 1981ª*

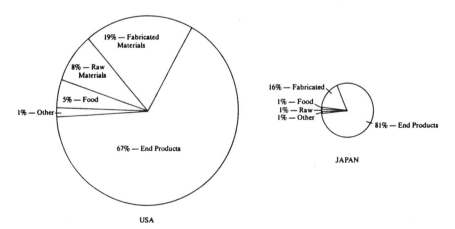

Table 2-7: *Trade Balance in Fabricated Materials and End Products*[a]

	($ million)	
	With USA	*With Japan*
1980	–9640	–1036
1975	–5727	–752
1970	–386	–283
1965	–1601	–137

Note
a. Source: Statistics Canada.

Direct Investment

Private direct investment between Canada and Japan has not kept pace with the enormous growth of trade between the two countries. Indeed, a striking feature of bilateral investment between Canada and Japan is the surprisingly small size of that investment, relative to the scale of the national economies involved and to the volume of trade.

Japanese licensed investment in Canada increased substantially during the 1970s and at a faster pace than that of most other investing countries. According to Japan's Ministry of Finance, accumulated investment (direct and portfolio) grew from only US$113 million in 1969 to US$1.25 billion (Can. $1.56 billion) as of March 1983. (See Figure 2-4.)

Despite its considerable growth record, Japanese investment in Canada has not kept pace with total Japanese investment overseas. From 1951 to 1970, the Canadian share of the total was nearly 6 per cent of all licensed Japanese foreign investment. For 1970 alone, when investment for that year nearly equalled the total of the previous two decades, it accounted for a remarkable 10.8 per cent of Japanese overseas investment. Since then, however, Canada has received a substantially smaller share. Canada now accounts for only 3 per cent of all outstanding Japanese foreign investment, ranking eighth in the scale of recipients.[3] Changing Japanese priorities account for that decrease. During the 1970s, world-wide Japanese investment in mining and forest products, the most important targets for investment in Canada, grew more slowly than total Japanese investment. The manufacturing sector, on the other hand, increased its share of the total, but that investment was largely directed towards the developing countries.

Although the extent of Japanese investment in Canada may seem large in absolute terms, it represents an extremely small proportion of total foreign investment in Canada. Data supplied by Statistics Canada on incoming foreign investment are available only to the end of 1979. As of that year, the cumulative Japanese investment represented

Figure 2-4: *Japanese Licensed Investment in Canada*
(million US dollars)

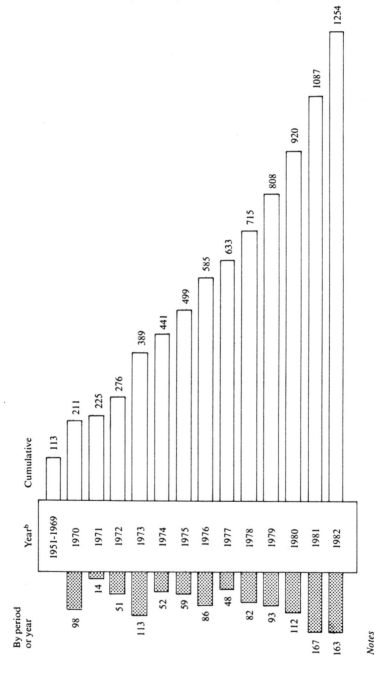

Notes

a. Source: Japanese Ministry of Finance.

b. Years refer to fiscal years. Fiscal year 1982 ended March 1983.

less than 1 per cent of all foreign direct investment in Canada. (See Table 2-8.) Recent approvals by the Foreign Investment Review Agency (FIRA) indicate a substantially higher level of Japanese investment since 1981, but that investment remains less than 1 per cent of the total value of direct investment allowed. Table 2-9 summarizes available data on the number and size of Japanese investment proposals approved by FIRA to the end of July 1983. Over the nine-and-one-half-year period reported, FIRA approved twenty-five acquisitions and sixty-one new-business applications from Japan, for a total reported investment value of $745 million, or approximately $8.7 million per application. It should be emphasized, however, that the Foreign Investment Review Act does *not* cover many of the types of investments which Japanese prefer, such as non-controlling equity positions and long-term loans.

Direct investment by Canadian companies in Japan is almost nonexistent. The total value of such investment was only $101 million as of 1980, reversing a trend of absolute decline through the late 1970s. (See Table 2-10.) Nearly all of the Canadian investment is in joint ventures with Japanese companies, largely in metal refining and metal products manufacturing. Reasons for the small Canadian investment include Japan's formal and implicit controls on foreign investment which have existed for many years, as well as complex cultural differences between Japan and the countries of North America.[4]

Special Characteristics of Japanese Investment[5]

Japanese investment is unlike traditional foreign investment in Canada. A high proportion of it is in the form of loans rather than equity, and the Japanese often take minority holdings or enter joint ventures. Another unique characteristic is the extensive participation of the large Japanese trading houses. In addition, while most foreign investment is destined for central Canada, most Japanese investment is earmarked for western Canada, particularly British Columbia and Alberta.

Just over half of Japanese investment in Canada is in equity. Most of the rest is in the form of loans, including corporate bonds and debentures, with a very small amount in real estate and in branches. This distribution almost exactly parallels that of Japan's world-wide investment, but differs markedly from the pattern of Japanese investment in the US, where 70 per cent is in equity. In forest products and metal fabricating, the chief focus of Japan's manufacturing investment in Canada, the ratio of loans to equity is higher

Table 2-8: *Foreign Direct Investment in Canada by Country of Origin*[a]

Year	USA			Japan			All Countries		
	$ million	% of total	Growth over Previous year	$ million	% of total	Growth over Previous year	$ million	% of total	Growth over Previous year
1979	42 800	79.0%	12%	500	0.9%	25%	54 200	100%	12%
1978	38 348	79.5%	2%	399	0.8%	19%	48 228	100%	3%
1977	37 602	80.1%	8%	335	0.7%	14%	46 951	100%	8%
1976	34 707	80.1%	8%	293	0.7%	14%	43 335	100%	8%
1975	32 251	80.4%	11%	258	0.6%	0%	40 137	100%	10%
1974	29 045	79.8%	11%	258	0.7%	3%	36 385	100%	11%
1973	26 143	79.5%	10%	250	0.8%	29%	32 873	100%	11%
1972	23 680	79.9%	6%	194	0.7%	4%	29 650	100%	6%
1971	22 443	80.1%	5%	187	0.7%	82%	28 003	100%	6%
1970	21 403	81.0%	7%	103	0.4%	47%	26 423	100%	8%
1969	19 959	81.8%	8%	70	0.3%	13%	24 400	100%	8%
1968	18 510	82.1%	9%	62	0.3%	82%	22 552	100%	9%
1967	17 000	82.1%	10%	34	0.2%	100%	20 710	100%	9%
1966	15 510	81.6%	10%	17	0.1%	70%	19 012	100%	10%
1965	14 059	81.0%	—	10	0.1%	—	17 356	100%	—

Notes
a. Source: Statistics Canada.

Table 2-9: *Number and Value of Cases from Japan Allowed to 31 July 1983*

	1974	1975	1976	1977	1978	1979	1980	1981	1982	1983 (July 31)	Total
Acquisitions:											
Number of cases	—	1	2	3	3	4	2	2	4	4	25
Value of assets ($ millions)	—	c^a	c	2.0	4.6	16.3	c	c	18.1	13.3	91.5
New Businesses											
Number of cases	—	—	4	5	5	9	2	8	14	14	61
Value of planned investment ($ millions)	—	—	11.8	1.0	c	2.0	c	280.6	306.6	50	653.5
Total											
Number of cases	—	1	6	8	8	13	4	10	18	18	86
Value of assets & planned investment ($ millions)	—	c	3.0	c	18.3	c	c	c	324.7	63.5	745.0

Note
a. The letter 'c' denotes confidential.

Table 2-10: *Canadian Direct Investment Abroad*[a]

	Investment in USA		Investment in Japan		Total Investment Abroad
	$ million	% of total	$ million	% of total	$ million
1980[b]	16 400	63.6	101	0.4	25 800
1979[b]	12 100	60.5	72	0.4	20 000
1978	8 898	54.7	63	0.4	16 253
1977	7 027	52.3	61	0.5	13 443
1976	6 092	53.0	68	0.6	11 501
1975	5 559	52.8	74	0.7	10 526
1974	4 909	53.3	77	0.8	9 201
1973	3 924	50.1	72	0.9	7 835
1972	3 431	51.1	71	1.1	6 715
1971	3 399	52.0	58	0.9	6 538
1970	3 251	52.5	48	0.8	6 188

Notes
a. Source: Statistics Canada.
b. Estimated figures.

than average, whereas in the principal non-manufacturing sectors, mining and trade, it is lower. In the trade sector, equity accounts for over 90 per cent of the investment.

Data supplied by Statistics Canada on the distribution of Japanese direct investment by industry sector are presented in Table 2-11. The data illustrate several significant changes in the directions of Japanese investments during the 1970s. Investment in merchandising, the largest recipient sector, grew rapidly in the early 1970s, reached a plateau in the middle of the decade, then began renewed rapid growth. The value of Japanese direct investment in manufacturing actually declined, from $115 million in 1973 to $106 million in 1979. The data show also a dramatic surge of investment activity in petroleum and natural gas in 1978, but new direct investment in that sector has since moderated, chiefly because of the introduction of Canada's new National Energy Policy.

It should be noted here that data released by Japan's Ministry of Finance on the size of Japanese investment in Canada differ substantially from those of Statistics Canada. The Japanese data:
• Are more current than Statistics Canada data
• Include all investment proposals authorized by the Japanese Ministry of Finance, whether realized or not
• Include portfolio as well as direct investments.
Consequently, investment figures reported from Japanese sources tend to be much larger than those from Canadian sources. Japanese Ministry of Finance data are more realistic and timely in an aggregate sense,

Table 2-11:[a] *Sectoral Distribution of Japanese Direct Investment in Canada ($ millions)*[b]

	Manufacturing	Petroleum and Gas	Mining	Merchandising	Financial	Other	Total
1979	106	83	61	171	15	43	479
1978	94	81	53	124	7	40	399
1977	98	11	83	102	8	34	336
1976	100	9	67	83	8	26	293
1975	104	3	78	51	8	13	257
1974	111		74	51	8	14	258
1973	115		72	49	4	10	250
1972	104		42	34	4	10	194
1971	97		58	24	3	5	187
1970[c]	57		26	12	3	5	103

Notes
a. Statistics Canada.
b. Direct investment covers investment in branches, subsidiaries and controlled companies.
c. Pre-1970 data not available.

Figure 2-5: *Cumulative Japanese Investment in Canada by Industry Sector, 1978.*
Comparative Data

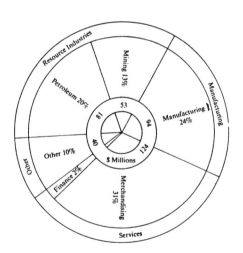

Source: Japanese Ministry of Finance.

Source: Statistics Canada.

but Statistics Canada data are more useful for analytic and comparative purposes. Figure 2-5 shows the industry distribution of Japanese investment in Canada as of 1978, using figures both from Statistics Canada and from the Japanese Ministry of Finance.

A Comparison of US and Japanese Business Involvement in Canada

Canadians' perceptions of and reactions to foreign-owned business activity are conditioned largely by their experience with American business. But the objectives, nature and scale of Japanese business involvement in Canada differ fundamentally from those of American firms. The differences are significant for Canadians.

The most obvious contrast between the Japanese and US presence in Canadian business is in sheer size. According to Statistics Canada, the 1979 value of US direct investment in Canada ($43 billion) was nearly *100 times* that of Japan's ($500 million). (See Table 2-8.) US business is also more highly focused, mainly on manufacturing and energy. The consequence, as most Canadians are painfully aware, is an overwhelming dominance of many of Canada's manufacturing and resource sectors by American-controlled firms, with consequent implications for Canada's economic sovereignty. Compared to US investment, Japanese investment in Canada is miniscule, and it is dispersed among the manufacturing, merchandising and resource sectors. The small size and absence of concentration of Japanese investment would seem to preclude any comparable threat of direct control by Japanese business, except in very limited sectors.

Significant differences exist also in the objectives and nature of Japanese and American investments in Canada. American companies, in their overseas involvements in general, have tended to seek to establish direct presence through the creation of controlled subsidiaries abroad. Japanese companies, in contrast, seek involvement mainly through the creation of trade links. While American investments, especially in manufacturing, are designed generally to maximize *cash* flows to the parent company, from sources such as dividends and royalties, Japanese investments are designed to maximize *trade* flows. For most Japanese companies, foreign direct investment has been undertaken only to the extent needed to secure supplies of materials flowing to Japan and to stimulate markets for Japanese-produced manufactures abroad. These objectives may be realized with minimal amounts of direct investment,[6] often through minority equity positions and indirect financing. These global differences hold true in Canada.

The Japanese preference for engaging Canadians in trade rather than in securing controlled investments in Canada appears vividly when we contrast relative investment and trade values for Japan and the USA. The 1979 trade volume between Canada and the USA ($88.9 billion) was 2.1 times the cumulative book value of US investment in Canada ($42.8 billion); whereas the value of Canada-Japan trade ($6.2 billion) was 12.5 times the value of Japanese investment ($500 million). (See Table 2-12.)

Table 2-12: *Relation of Trade and Investment Values, 1979 ($ million)*[a]

	USA	Japan
Cumulative direct investment value from:	42 800	500
Canadian exports to:	43 463	4 077
Canadian imports from:	45 420	2 157
Total bilateral trade with:	88 883	6 234
Trade as % of investment:	*2.1 times*	*12.5 times*

Note
a. Source: Statistics Canada.

Statistical information comparing the use of joint ventures and indirect financing between Japanese and American firms in Canada is unavailable. But the greater Japanese tendency toward indirect participation through loans and other portfolio investments is reflected in the contrasting patterns of payments flowing back from Canada. Table 2-13 compares the relationship of interest and dividend flows from Japanese and American *direct* investments with corresponding flows from *portfolio* investments. Except for 1981, when there was an abnormally high outflow of payments from Japanese direct investments, the Japanese have consistently received a higher proportion of payments from portfolio investments in Canada than have US firms, and relatively less from direct investments. Figure 2-6 summarizes the composition of overall payments flows from Canada to Japan and the USA for 1979, the most recent year for which complete information is available. Significantly, 64 per cent of payments to Japan were in the form of interest, with only 33 per cent in dividends and 1 per cent in royalties. In contrast, the bulk of payments flows to the USA were dividends, which stood at 46 per cent, and royalties, which stood at 12 per cent, with only 9 per cent in interest.

Table 2-13: *Investment Income Payments ($ million)*[a]

	Japan			USA			All Countries		
	Direct	*Portfolio*	*%*[b]	*Direct*	*Portfolio*	*%*[b]	*Direct*	*Portfolio*	*%*[b]
1981	69	106	65	2 325	3 413	68	2 835	5 270	54
1980	13	73	18	1 952	3 085	63	2 279	4 682	49
1979	14	56	25	2 045	2 810	73	2 294	4 218	54
1978	10	28	36	1 836	2 445	75	2 258	3 646	62
1977	8	12	67	1 397	2 007	70	1 595	2 937	54

Notes
a. Source: Statistics Canada.
b. Direct investment income payments as a per cent of portfolio investment income payments.

Figure 2-6: *Canadian Payments to USA and Japan, 1979ª*

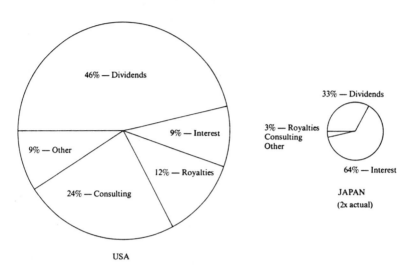

USA

JAPAN
(2x actual)

Summary

Trade between Canada and Japan has grown dramatically in recent years, in value and in terms of its importance to both countries. On the surface, the trade relationship appears satisfactory to Canadians: the overall balance is consistently in Canada's favour. But Canadians have reasons for apprehension, both with short-term developments and with underlying structural characteristics. The size of the Canadian surplus on bilateral trade shrank drastically during 1980 and 1981, both because of a slow-down of growth in Japanese demand for Canadian raw materials, and because of a substantial increase in the import of Japanese autos, which competes directly with a depressed domestic auto industry. This immediate crisis is only one manifestation of a more fundamental qualitative imbalance in trade between the two countries: Canadian exports to Japan are mainly raw materials and commodities, whereas imports from Japan are almost exclusively manufactured products. This qualitative imbalance, which leaves Canada in the position of a less-developed country in relation to Japan, appears to be increasing, rather than decreasing. Mistrust and acrimony are bound to grow unless the Japanese take significant steps to upgrade the processing of raw materials before they leave Canada; to obtain more auto parts and other manufactured components from Canada; and to impose more orderly control on exports to Canada of

Japanese-manufactured products which threaten to displace existing Canadian industries. These are all feasible steps which the Japanese could take at minimal cost to themselves.

Japanese direct investment in Canada is small in relation to total foreign investment. Unlike other investors, who generally seek to gain direct control of affiliated companies in Canada, Japanese investors aim primarily to secure reliable flows of raw materials to Japan and to facilitate the export sale of products manufactured in Japan. As a consequence, Japanese investment in Canada has unique characteristics: it is focused mainly on natural resources and merchandising, rather than on manufacturing; it emphasizes long-term loans and minority-equity positions, rather than control; and it flows largely to western Canada, rather than to the country's industrial heartland. In their willingness to provide needed financing and markets, without seeking to establish control, the Japanese aims seem compatible with Canada's stated objectives of welcoming foreign participation which does not threaten national economic sovereignty. The problem is that only a very small portion of the Japanese investment is directed toward manufacturing or processing activities which would maximize domestic job creation and value added. Instead of just moving energy and raw materials to the site of Japanese industry, it is time, in the view of many Canadians, for the Japanese to become more willing to move some of their processing and manufacturing to the site of the resources they use.

Notes

1. "Japanese Promise 25 per cent cut in sales of cars to Canada," Toronto *Globe and Mail,* 12 August 1982, p. 1.

2. "Sales of Autos from Japan Off," *Globe and Mail* 12 August 1983, p. B8. See also "Imported car sales slip in August," *Globe and Mail,* 15 September 1982, p. B4, and "Nissan planning to sell subcompact car in '84," *Globe and Mail,* 23 September 1983, p. B2.

3. Joan Gherson, "Japanese Investment in Canada."

4. Richard W. Wright, "Canadian Joint Ventures in Japan." In the author's view, the nature and treatment of Canadian investment in Japan has little relationship with Japanese business investment in Canada; consequently the topic will not be dealt with further in this book.

5. The author is grateful to Joan Gherson for some of the ideas developed in this section. See Gherson, "Japanese Investment." Also Richard W. Wright, "Japan's Investment in Canada."

6. The distinction between direct investment and portfolio or indirect investment is explained further in Chapter 3.

3: Japanese Business in Canada

Japanese business firms enter Canada for a variety of purposes, and their involvement takes many forms. In this study their activities are classified in five broad categories.

- *Energy and Resources:* Activities of Japanese-controlled companies involved in exploring, extracting, processing and other resource-based activities in Canada, primarily to obtain materials for export to Japan
- *Merchandising:* Activities of Canadian subsidiaries of Japanese manufacturing companies, engaged primarily in importing and selling their Japanese-made products in Canada
- *Trade:* Activities of the general and specialized Japanese trading companies in Canada, engaged in importing and exporting commodities or processed products of other companies
- *Manufacturing:* Activities of Japanese-controlled companies in Canada whose main activity is the manufacture of industrial or consumer products for sale domestically or elsewhere
- *Services:* Activities of Japanese-controlled financial institutions and other service-oriented companies in Canada.

In this chapter, the activities of Japanese businesses in Canada are described under each of these categories, and their direct economic effects are summarized. Total induced impact and its regional distribution are discussed in Chapter 4. Other non-quantifiable effects are discussed in Chapter 5.

Identification and Classification

The lists of Japanese businesses in Canada that are contained in this report were derived from a variety of sources and are believed to be the most comprehensive ever compiled. Two sources were of prime im-

31

portance: the lists of foreign-controlled corporations, by nationality of origin, published by Statistics Canada in *Inter-Corporate Ownership;*[1] and *Japanese Overseas Investment: A Complete Listing by Firms and Countries,* the directory of Japanese investments abroad, by country of destination, published annually by *The Oriental Economist.*[2] The former has the advantage of tracing not only direct foreign ownership of businesses in Canada, but also indirect or ultimate ownership. Where, for example, a company in Canada is controlled by a Canadian-incorporated holding company or other subsidiary which, in turn, is controlled from Japan, *Inter-Corporate Ownership* will reveal the final or ultimate extent of foreign control. Wherever possible, ownership figures reported in this study represent *ultimate,* rather than immediate, control. *The Oriental Economist* information has the advantage of revealing additional details not disclosed in *Inter-Corporate Ownership,* such as nature of activity, sales volume, and number of employees. Both sources are, regrettably, incomplete. Data from these sources were supplemented by extensive interviews with more than fifty corporate executives and public officials, as well as by published data from a variety of other sources. In those few instances where direct information appeared to be unobtainable, missing data (such as number of employees) were extrapolated from available data (such as sales volume), in proportion to the patterns of other related companies. As data pertaining to individual companies were often supplied in confidence, data presented throughout this report are clustered to maintain confidentiality.

It should be emphasized that the discussion and statistical analysis of this and subsequent chapters is confined to *direct* investments in Canada by Japanese firms. There is no uniformly accepted definition of direct investment. Conceptually, any company supplying a sufficient quantity of equity and/or long-term debt capital to have a 'significant' role in the management of an affiliated company should be considered a direct investor, as opposed to an arm's-length portfolio investor. *For purposes of this study, Japanese participation was deemed to constitute direct investment where 20 per cent or more of the equity of a Canadian affiliate is controlled ultimately from Japan.* The analysis includes only firms of at least $10 000 assets or $5 000 sales. *All* known Canadian businesses of this size controlled at least 50 per cent from Japan are included, as well as most such firms with 20-49 per cent Japanese control. (Some small firms in the 20-49 per cent ownership range were excluded because of difficulty in obtaining information, and because their inclusion would have been insignificant to the statistical results.)

In many instances, Japanese business firms engage in activities in more than one of the categories used here. Often separate subsidiaries are created in such circumstances. For example, most of the large general trading companies engage not only in the purchase and resale of Canadian raw materials, but also in their mining and extraction. In most such instances, separate mining companies have been created (usually jointly with Canadian interests), most of which sell their output to the affiliated trading companies. Similarly, among the Japanese merchandising affiliates in Canada are several which conduct significant manufacturing or assembly operations. In several such operations, the manufacturing is conducted by a separate organizational entity from the sales activity. Under such arrangements, the activities and effects even of diversified companies may reasonably be allocated among the categories used here.

In other instances, however, category assignments are less clear. It is especially difficult to define exactly when certain resource-related activities should be classifed as manufacturing. Most of the Japanese forestry-products companies perform milling as well as logging operations in Canada; consequently they are included here as manufacturers. Similarly, a number of the Japanese fishery companies perform canning operations in Canada. But partly because of the small scale of their operations and the difficulty of gaining information about them, they are all classified here as resource-related companies, rather than as manufacturers. The author acknowledges that the categorization of firms is highly subjective. He believes, nonetheless, that the total impact of direct Japanese business activity in Canada is captured to a sufficient extent within the overall analysis.

Energy and Resources

A number of Japanese business firms have come to Canada to secure primary resources such as fuels, metals, forestry products, and food products. Their activities, ranging from exploration to extraction to processing, may be clustered into three main sub-sectors:

- *Exploration and mining.* Japanese firms participate in at least twenty Canadian affiliates engaged in exploration and mining activities. At the time of writing, only one of the companies of this group (B.C. Coal Ltd.) had more than twelve employees, and it had over 2000. Most of the other companies consist essentially of representative offices serving a liaison function between their Japanese parent firms and Canadian-based energy and mining companies. Many have only a handful of employees and make no direct sales, and thus their *direct* economic impact in terms of employment and local purchases appears negligible. Their liaison role is, nonetheless, an important one. The local Japanese presence in representative offices facilitates communication between the Japanese and Canadian interests, and expedites contract negotiations and procurement procedures.

- *Forestry products.* By far the largest direct economic impact of Japanese-controlled business in the resource sectors is in forestry products, concentrated in British Columbia. The Japanese activity ranges from logging to the operation of several large mills manufacturing pulp, lumber and plywood. (Because of their quasi-manufacturing nature, their impact is discussed and measured in the section on Manufacturing.)

- *Agricultural and Fishing Products.* Other resource-related activities of Japanese businesses in Canada include several small companies involved in harvesting and canning fish products and three firms processing rapeseed oil. (These last are included in the Manufacturing section.)

The tendency for Japanese companies to invest in minority equity positions in Canadian-controlled companies, rather than in subsidiaries wholly- or majority-controlled from Japan, is particularly evident in the energy and resource sectors. There are two main explanations for this pattern, as follows.

- *Nationalistic pressures and controls.* Even at the time of the earliest Japanese investments, when few formal controls existed, attempts by Japanese companies to acquire direct control of major natural-resource deposits might have generated embarrassing and potentially restrictive nationalistic feelings on the part of Canadians. More recently, the creation of the Foreign Investment Review Agency (FIRA) has placed requirements for formal screening and approval on potential attempts by Japanese firms (as well as other foreign firms) to secure controlling interests. Still further barriers have been created by Canada's National Energy Policy (NEP), which established new Canadian-ownership requirements in energy-related resource sectors.

- *Materials-supply objectives.* Even in the absence of formal controls or pressures, the evidence is strong that Japanese companies would prefer to participate in the resource sectors through minority-partnership positions. As discussed earlier in this report, priority objectives of Japanese participation are to stimulate the development of new sources of raw materials and to gain rights to purchase the materials produced. Minority-partnership participation provides a sufficiently close link between the Japanese and Canadian partners to ensure achievement of these objectives, while maintaining a low profile and avoiding difficult day-to-day management decisions.

Since Japan's investment in resources is motivated mainly by its industry's needs for raw materials, its targets in Canada's resource sectors have shifted over time.[3] During the 1960s, copper was particularly attractive to Japanese investors, who took minority positions in a number of developments in British Columbia, often providing debt financing and long-term sales contracts. Most Japanese investments in the forest industry were made between 1967 and 1973; during this period, Japanese interests gained control of several sawmills and pulp-and-lumber companies, all located in British Columbia. By the early 1970s, investor interest focused on metallurgical coal in order to provide assured supplies for Japan's fast-growing steel industry. Since the mid-1970s, higher oil prices have sparked Japanese participation in Arctic petroleum exploration and in non-conventional oil resources in Alberta, mainly through massive long-term loans. The Japanese are also engaging in exploration for uranium, reflecting their substantial commitment to nuclear energy for generating electricity. Major projects planned or under discussion for the future include Japanese participation in the development of northern British Columbia coal deposits, liquified natural gas, and petrochemicals. (See Chapters 5 and 6.)

Table 3-1 lists thirty-nine resources-related companies in Canada, in which at least 20 per cent of the equity is controlled ultimately by Japanese. Excluding the firms that deal in forestry products and vegetable oil, whose impact is included in the Manufacturing subsection, the remaining firms, taken together, employed 3400 people in 1981, mostly in coal mining in British Columbia. This total may seem surprisingly low in light of Japan's prominence in Canadian resource developments. It should be recalled, however, that *direct* Japanese investment, measured here, is mainly in exploration projects or liaison offices, with few employees. Japanese firms participate in a number of additional Canadian resource companies through loans or equity holdings lower than 20 per cent. As such positions are generally regarded as portfolio investments rather than direct investments, their economic effects are not quantified in this section. This does not mean that they are unimportant. Indeed, many resource-related projects of substantial importance to Canada might not have been undertaken had it not been for the portfolio financing or other indirect participation of Japanese firms. In such instances, the total employment and value-added benefits of the project could justifiably be attributed to the Japanese. It is, however, difficult, if not impossible, to judge on a case-by-case basis whether or not such projects would have been undertaken in the absence of the Japanese participation. For consistency, the effects of all operations with less than 20 per cent Japanese equity ownership are excluded entirely. Some qualitative aspects of Japanese loan financing and purchase contracts are discussed further in Chapter 5.

Table 3-1: *Resource-Related Companies*

Company Name	Province	Ultimate Japanese Ownership (%)	Activity
Subgroup A: Exploration and Mining			
Alpac Aluminium Limited	Quebec	50	Aluminium refining & sales
B.C. Coal Ltd.	BC	33	Coal mining & sales
Deas Lake Mines Ltd.	BC	44	Copper-mine development
Domik Exploration Limited	Ontario	100	Non-ferrous metal exploration
Dowa Mining Co. Ltd.	BC	100	Prospecting
Japan Canada Oil Sands Ltd.	Alberta	100	Oil exploration
Japan Oil Sands Co. Primrose Ltd.	Alberta	100	Oil & natural gas exploration
Japex Canada Ltd.	Alberta	100	Oil exploration
Kaiser Coal Canada Ltd.	BC	25	Coal mining & sales
Koizumi Group (Canada) Ltd.	Quebec	100	Mica mining
Mitsui Coal Development (Canada) Ltd.	Alberta	100	Coal-mine development
Mitsui Mining Canada Ltd.	BC	100	Mineral exploration
Nippon Mining of Canada Ltd.	BC	100	Mineral exploration
PNC Exploration (Canada) Ltd.	BC	100	Mineral exploration
Pacific Coal Limited	BC	70	Coal development
Polychrome Corporation Canada Ltd.	Ontario	100	Prospecting
Quintette Coal Ltd.	BC	50	Coal mining
Southeast Asia Bauxites Ltd.	Quebec	25	Bauxite exploration & sales
Sumac Mines Ltd.	BC	100	Non-ferrous metal development
Sumitomo Metal Mining (Canada) Ltd.	BC	100	Non-ferrous metal exploration
Subgroup B: Forestry and Forest Products			
CIPA Industries Ltd.[a]	BC	100	Logging and lumber
Cariboo Pulp & Paper Ltd.[a]	BC	50	Pulp and paper

Table 3-1 continued

Company Name	Province	Ultimate Japanese Ownership (%)	Activity
Crestbrook Forest Industries Ltd.[a]	BC	54	Pulp, lumber & plywood
Diashowa-Marubeni International Ltd.[a]	BC	100	Pulp
Mayo Forest Products Ltd.[a]	BC	40	Lumber
Naden Harbour Timber Ltd.[a]	BC	100	Logging
New Brunswick International Paper Co.[a]	NB	33	Paper
Quesnel River Pulp Co.[a]	BC	50	Pulp
Subgroup C: Agricultural and Fishery Products			
Aero International Enterprises Ltd.	BC	100	Food products
Alberta Food Products[a]	Alberta	40	Vegetable oil
Atlantic Ocean Products Ltd.	Nfld.	49	Fish products
Cassiar Packing Co. Ltd.	BC	50	Fish Products
Japan-Alberta Oil Mill Co. Ltd.[a]	Alberta	100	Vegetable Oil
Lakeside Farm Industries Ltd.	Alberta	20	Cattle breeding
Nippon Suisan (Canada) Ltd.	BC	100	Fish products
Richocean Trading Company Ltd.	NS	100	Fish products
Taiyo Canada Limited	Nfld.	100	Fish products
Tonquin Enterprises	BC	20	Fish processing
United Oilseed Products[a]	Alberta	33	Vegetable oil

Note

a. Economic effects included under manufacturing.

Merchandising

By far the largest number of Japanese-controlled businesses in Canada are subsidiaries of Japanese manufacturing companies, set up to distribute their products in Canada. Some seventy Japanese manufacturers have major sales-oriented subsidiaries in Canada. Some of them sell industrial products, but most distribute Japanese-made consumer products whose names are well known.

Among the largest Japanese employers of Canadians are the automobile companies. Although considerable attention has been focused on the loss of jobs in the Canadian auto industry resulting from the import of Japanese-made autos, a large number of Canadians are employed in the various phases of importing, transporting and selling Japanese cars in Canada. The four largest Japanese auto importers— Honda, Mazda, Nissan, and Toyota—employ 760 Canadians in their Canadian-headquarters operations alone. Even this is only the tip of the iceberg. There are 937 Canadian dealers in Japanese automobiles, who in 1981 employed more than 12 200 people. Gross wages paid by these dealers in the same period were $240 million, and their investment in plant and equipment at the end of 1981 amounted to $558 million.[4] Most of the dealerships are controlled by Canadians, however, and their economic impact is therefore excluded from the present analysis.[5]

Nearly all of the Canadian merchandising affiliates of Japanese manufacturing companies are located in Ontario, and most are wholly owned by the Japanese parent. A listing by size group is presented as Table 3-2. Most of the distributing companies are small: forty-one of the sixty-four employ fewer than fifty employees. Of the twelve companies employing one hundred or more people, most are well-known Japanese manufacturers of consumer goods such as automobiles (Honda, Nissan, Toyota, Yamaha); electronics and electrical appliances (Matsushita, Sony, Hitachi, Toshiba); cameras (Canon); and watches (Seiko).

Trading

The Japanese trading companies represent some of the oldest Japanese investments in Canada, many dating from the early 1950s, when they first began to establish themselves around the world. All nine of the large Japanese general trading companies *(Sogo-shosha)* are represented, most with multiple branches across Canada, as well as a number of smaller, more specialized, trading companies. (See Table 3-3.)

Table 3-2: *Merchandising Companies*

Company Name	Province	Ultimate Japanese Ownership (%)	Activity
Subgroup A: 200 or more Employees			
Canon Optics & Business Machines Canada Ltd.	Ontario	90	Optical devices & business machines
Consolidated Computer Inc.	Ontario	24	Business-information systems
Honda Canada Inc.	Ontario	100	Motor-vehicle sales
Matsushita Electric of Canada Ltd.	Ontario	100	Electrical products sales
Nissan Automobile Co. Canada Ltd.	BC	100	Motor-vehicle sales
Sony of Canada Ltd.	Man.	49	Electronics-products sales
Toyota Canada Inc.	Ontario	100	Motor-vehicle sales
Subgroup B: 100-199 Employees			
Hitachi (HSC) Canada Inc.	Quebec	100	Household-appliances sales
Seiko Time Canada Ltd.	Ontario	100	Watch sales
Toshiba of Canada Ltd.	Ontario	100	Home-appliances sales
Yamaha Canada Music Ltd.	Ontario	100	Musical instruments sales
Yamaha Motor Canada Ltd.	Ontario	100	Motor-bike sales
Subgroup C: 50-99 Employees			
Akai Canada, Inc.	BC	49	Audio-visual products sales
Alspeed Products Limited	Ontario	100	Chain-saw sales
Brother International Corp. Canada Ltd.	Quebec	100	Sewing & knitting-machine sales
Canadian Kawasaki Motors Ltd.	Ontario	100	Motorcycles & snowmobiles sales
Daiwa (Canada) Ltd.	BC	48	Fishing & sporting-goods sales
Fuji Photo Film Canada Inc.	Quebec	67	Film and camera sales
Mazda Canada Inc.	Ontario	100	Motor-vehicle sales

Table 3-2 continued

Company Name	Province	Ultimate Japanese Ownership (%)	Activity
Nikon Canada Inc.	Quebec	49	Camera sales
Pentax of Canada Ltd.	BC	100	Cameras & optical equipment sales
Sharp Electronics of Canada Ltd.	Ontario	100	Electronics-product sales
Suzuki Canada Inc.	Ontario	100	Motor-vehicle sales
Subgroup D: 25-49 Employees			
Bell & Howell/ Mamiya Co. Canada Ltd.	Ontario	50	Photographic equipment sales
Bridgestone Tire Co. of Canada Ltd.	BC	50	Automobile-tires and tube sales
Canadian Koyo Co. Ltd.	Ontario	100	Bearings sales
JVC Canada Inc.	Ontario	100	Electrical products sales
Komatsu Canada Ltd.	Ontario	100	Tractor sales
Kubota Tractor Canada Ltd.	Ontario	100	Tractor sales
Makita Power Tools Canada Ltd.	Ontario	100	Electric power-tools sales
NTN Bearing Corporation of Canada Ltd.	Ontario	100	Bearings sales
Noritake Canada Ltd.	Ontario	90	Chinaware sales
Spectro Electric Industry Inc.	Ontario	50	Electronics-product sales
Subgroup E: 10-24 Employees			
Elmo Canada Manufacturing Corp.	Ontario	100	Projector sales
Hitachi Construction Machinery Canada Ltd.	Ontario	100	Construction-machinery sales
Hitachi-Denshi Ltd.	Ontario	100	Electronic-product sales
Janome Sewing Machine Co. (Canada) Ltd.	Ontario	75	Sewing-machine sales
Japan Food Corp. (Canada) Ltd.	Ontario	40	Import & sales of Japanese food
Lux Audio of Canada Ltd.	Ontario	50	Audio-equipment sales
MBL Sales Ltd.	Alberta	100	Industrial belt sales
MKB Music Ltd.	Man.	100	Piano and organ sales

Table 3-2 continued

Company Name	Province	Ultimate Japanese Ownership (%)	Activity
Minolta Business Equipment Canada Ltd.	Ontario	100	Business-equipment sales
NSK Bearing Canada Ltd.	Ontario	100	Bearings sales
Pulsar Time Canada Inc.	Ontario	100	Watch sales
Tokyo Electric Canada Ltd.	Ontario	100	Sales of electrical equipment
Yashika Canada Inc.	Ontario	100	Photo & optical equipment sales
Subgroup F: Fewer than 10 Employees			
Alpine Electronics of Canada Inc.	Ontario	100	Electronics-products sales
Asahi Chemical Industry Canada Ltd.	Ontario	100	Chemical products sales
C. Itoh Industrial Machinery Canada Ltd.	Ontario	100	Machinery & equipment sales
Hitachi (Canadian) Ltd.	Ontario	100	Holding company
Ken Parisien Pianos Ltd.	Ontario	100	Musical instrument sales
Marubeni Construction Machinery Canada Ltd.	Ontario	100	Construction-machinery sales
Mita Copystar Canada	Ontario	100	Copying-machine sales
Mycom Canada Limited	BC	100	Industrial refrigerator sales
NKG Insulators of Canada Ltd.	Ontario	99	Insulators sales
Nachi Canada	Ontario	100	Bearings sales
Nippondenso Canada Ltd.	Ontario	100	Automobile parts & air conditioners
Rapifax of Canada Ltd.	BC	100	Telecommunications-equipment sales
Sumiglass Products Ltd.	BC	100	Sheet glass sales
Tablework KS Ltd.	Ontario	70	Chinaware sales
Takara Company (Canada) Ltd.	Ontario	100	Furniture sales
Torcan-KDK International Co. Ltd.	Ontario	73	Electrical appliances sales
Toshiba International Corp. (Cdn. Br.)	Ontario	100	Electrical products sales
Yokohama Tire Corporation	BC	100	Automotive tire sales

Table 3-3: *Trading Companies*

Company Name	Main Office	Regional Offices
Subgroup A: General Trading Companies		
C. Itoh & Co. (Canada) Ltd.	Calgary	Montreal, Toronto, Vancouver
Kanematsu-Gosho (Canada) Ltd.	Toronto	Montreal, Calgary, Vancouver
Marubeni Canada Ltd.	Toronto	Montreal, Calgary, Vancouver
Mitsubishi Canada Ltd.	Vancouver	Montreal, Toronto, Calgary
Mitsui & Co. Canada Ltd.	Toronto	Montreal, Calgary, Vancouver
Nichimen Canada Ltd.	Montreal	
Nissho-Iwai Canada Ltd.	Toronto	Montreal, Calgary, Vancouver
Sumitomo Canada Ltd.	Vancouver	Montreal, Calgary
Toyomenka Canada Inc.	Toronto	Montreal, Vancouver
Subgroup B: Others		
Chori Canada Ltd.	Montreal	Toronto
CTC Trading Ltd.	Vancouver	
Diahakone Kankoo-Jigyo Co. Ltd.	Vancouver	
Fuji Trading Co. Ltd.	Vancouver	
Itoman (Canada) Inc.	Montreal	
J. Osawa Canada Inc.	Toronto	
Kawasho International Canada Ltd.	Vancouver	
Misawa Homes of Canada Ltd.	Winnipeg	
Nichimo Trading Co. Ltd.	Vancouver	
Nozaki Trading Inc.	Vancouver	
Okura & Company Canada Ltd.	Vancouver	
Sato Canada Trading Inc.	Vancouver	
Shinko Canada Ltd.	Montreal	
Toshoku Canada Ltd.	Vancouver	
Tsuda Canada Ltd.	Vancouver	
Yuasa Shoji Co. Ltd.	Vancouver	Toronto

The trading companies play at least three major roles in Canada. Their principal function is the export of Canadian resources and materials, mainly to Japan.[6] A second is to serve as wholesaler for a wide range of Japanese-made products imported into Canada. A third function is to participate directly in various mining and processing activities, mainly through joint ventures with other Japanese or Canadian partners.

The direct economic impact of the trading companies—measured narrowly in terms of direct employment and consumption of goods and services—appears relatively small: the nine large general trading companies together employ only 596 people in their offices across Canada. But their importance in generating trade and stimulating investment in Canada can hardly be overstated. A more detailed description of these indirect impacts is contained in Chapter 5 of this study.

Manufacturing

Except in forestry products, Canada has not been as successful as Europe or the United States in attracting Japanese capital in manufacturing. However, the few Japanese companies which do manufacture in Canada (see Table 3-4), produce a variety of products, and several generate significant exports from Canada.

The manufacturing activities of Japanese companies in Canada tend to fall into two distinct categories: those involving the processing of primary goods prior to their export to Japan or elsewhere; and those involving the manufacture or assembly of consumer and industrial end products, mainly for the domestic Canadian market. Activities in the first category focus almost entirely on the manufacture of pulp, paper, timber, plywood, and other forestry products. Agriculture-related manufacturing is limited to three plants producing rapeseed oil, plus some small fish-canning operations. Virtually no significant processing has been undertaken in the other natural resource sectors such as non-ferrous metals.

Reasons cited for the modest Japanese effort to manufacture consumer and industrial products in Canada include:

- The small size and relative saturation of the domestic Canadian market
- High production costs which preclude significant manufacturing for export to other markets
- The unsatisfactory profit performance and recent failures of several existing investments.

Japanese investment in end-product manufacturing in Canada actually declined through much of the 1970s, as the result of a number of bankruptcies or divestments, most notably in the manufacturing of textiles.

Table 3-4 lists eighteen Japanese manufacturing companies in Canada. Together they employ nearly 4700 people in Canada. About 60 per cent of that total, that is, 2841 people, are employed in the forestry-products sector, almost exclusively in British Columbia and New Brunswick. Most of the remainder, that is, 1225 employees, work at the production of TVs, stereos, and other household electrical appliances; this activity is focused in Ontario and Quebec.

Services

A variety of services are performed by Japanese companies in Canada, mainly in tourism and finance. (See Table 3-5.) The largest individual employer of Canadians in this sector is the Japanese-owned Prince Hotel in Toronto, with 400 employees, followed by Japan Airlines, with 162 employees. Japanese banks and other financial institutions together employ an additional 175 people. A discussion of the changing position of Japanese banks in Canada is included in Chapter 5.

Table 3-4: *Manufacturing Companies*

Company Name	Province	Ultimate Japanese Ownership (%)	Activity
Subgroup A: Agricultural Products			
Alberta Food Products	Alberta	40	Vegetable oil
Japan-Alberta Oil Mill Co. Ltd.	Alberta	100	Vegetable oil
United Oilseed Products Ltd.	Alberta	33	Vegetable oil
Subgroup B: Forestry and Forest Products			
CIPA Industries Ltd.	BC	100	Logging and lumber
Cariboo Pulp & Paper Ltd.	BC	50	Pulp and paper
Crestbrook Forest Industries Ltd.	BC	54	Pulp, lumber & plywood
Diashowa-Marubeni International Ltd.	BC	100	Pulp
Mayo Forest Products Ltd.	BC	40	Lumber
Naden Harbour Timber Ltd.	BC	100	Logging
New Brunswick International Paper Co.	NB	33	Paper
Quesnel River Pulp Co.	BC	50	Pulp
Subgroup C: Consumer and Industrial Products			
Erie Technological Products Ltd.	Ontario	100	Manufacture of electronic parts
Hitachi Canada Inc.	Ontario	100	Manufacture of household appliances
Matsushita Industrial Canada Ltd.	Ontario	100	Manufacture of color TVs and stereos
NTN Bearing Mfg. Canada Ltd.	Ontario	87	Ball-bearing manufacturer
Sanyo Canada Inc.	Quebec	50	Manufacture of TVs and stereos
Titan Steel and Wire Co. Ltd.	BC	61	Steel-wire manufacture
YKK Canada Ltd.	Quebec	100	Manufacture of zippers & fasteners

Table 3-5: *Service Companies*

Company Name	Province	Ultimate Japanese Ownership (%)	Activity
Subgroup A: Banks			
Bank of Tokyo	Ont./Alta./BC	100	Commercial banking services
Dai-Ichi Kangyo Bank	Ontario	100	Commercial banking services
Daiwa Bank	Ontario	100	Bank representative office
Fuji Bank	Ontario	100	Commercial banking services
Industrial Bank of Japan	Ontario	100	Commercial banking services
Long Term Credit Bank	Ontario	100	Bank representative office
Mitsubishi Bank	Ont./BC	100	Commercial banking services
Mitsui Bank	Ontario	100	Commercial banking services
Sanwa Bank	Ontario	100	Bank representative office
Sumitomo Bank	Ontario	100	Bank representative office
Taiyo Kobe Bank	Ontario	100	Bank representative office
Tokai Bank	Ontario	100	Bank representative office
Subgroup B: Other Financial Institutions			
Daiwa Securities Co. Ltd.	Ontario	100	Securities
Hitachi Credit Canada Ltd.	Ontario	60	Financing
Nissan Leasing Ltd.	BC	100	Financing
Nomura Securities Co. Ltd.	Ontario	100	Securities
Tokio Marine & Fire Insurance Co. Ltd.	Ontario	100	Insurance
Yamaichi International Canada Ltd.	Quebec	100	Securities
Yashuda Fire & Marine Insurance Co. Ltd.	Ontario	100	Insurance
Subgroup C: Other Services			
Canadian Hitachi Plant Construction Co.	Ontario	100	Building construction
Fraser Wharves Ltd.	BC	100	Auto storage & transport
Himac Motors Ltd.	BC	98	Truck assembly
Japan Airlines	BC	100	Transportation
Japan Line Ltd.	Ontario	100	Transportation
Marc-Narod Enterprises Ltd.	BC	100	Housing construction & sales
Prince Hotel Toronto Ltd.	Ontario	100	Hotel
Seibu Canada Ltd.	Ontario	100	Real estate
Shehiro Food Co. Ltd. (Canada)	Ontario	60	Restaurants
Yamachita-Shinnihon Steamship Co. Ltd.	Ontario	100	Transportation

Summary

Table 3-6 summarizes the direct employment effects of the 160 companies listed in this chapter, by activity and by province. These companies directly employed a total of 13 419 people in Canada at the end of 1981. The largest employment group was manufacturing, which employed 4667 people; it was followed closely by merchandising, which employed 4029 people, and resources, which employed 3390 people. Note, however, that all 2841 forestry-products employees and 155 rapeseed-oil employees are categorized here under manufacturing. If they were classified instead under resource industries, then the resource companies would constitute by far the largest group of employers with 6386 employees, or 47.6 per cent of the total number; manufacturing would represent a distant third, with 1671 employees or 12.5 per cent.

Table 3-6 also shows the geographical distribution of direct employment. British Columbia accounts for by far the largest amount of direct employment, with 5970 people or 44.4 per cent of the national total. Although most of this BC employment is in the resource industries, there is also substantial employment generated there in merchandising, trading and manufacturing (assuming that the production of forestry products is considered as manufacturing). The second-largest province of direct employment is Ontario, with 4274 employees; most of the merchandising companies and banks are located there. The 1174 Quebec employees are diversified among merchandising, trading and manufacturing. Nearly all of the Maritimes' employment of 1230 people is generated by forestry (pulp) manufacturing in New Brunswick. Japanese businesses employ about 400 people in Alberta, mostly in raising cattle and producing rapeseed; they employ an equal number in Manitoba, almost entirely in merchandising. Direct employment is virtually nil in Newfoundland, Nova Scotia, Prince Edward Island, Saskatchewan, and the Territories.

Table 3-7 presents aggregate data on direct employment, wage payments, and value added for firms in each of the five main categories. Direct employment figures were compiled from a combination of published sources and personal interviews, as decribed earlier in this chapter. Estimates of direct wages and salaries, and of direct value added, were computed from the Statistics Canada National Input-Output Model, using average Canadian ratios for wages and output per employee for each of the activities specified.[7]

According to these estimates, the Japanese companies paid out gross wages and salaries of $225.7 million in Canada in 1981, 44 per cent of which was earned in the manufacturing sector (including forest products). The total direct value added by the same companies was $387.6

Table 3-6: *Direct Employment of Japanese Companies, 1981*

		Maritimes	Quebec	Ontario	Man./Sask.	Alberta	BC	Canada
Group A:	*Energy & Resource Companies*							
	Mining & exploration		8	3		11	2 778	2 800
	Fish products	6					444	450
	Cattle					140		140
	Subtotal							3 390
Group B:	*Merchandising Companies*		437	2 626	396	15	555	4 029
Group C:	*Trading Companies*		134	185	3	49	225	596
Group D:	*Manufacturing Companies*							
	Rapeseed oil	1 224				155		155
	Forestry products						1 617	2 841
	TV and stereos		140	255				395
	Household appliances		250	580				830
	Ball bearings			75				75
	Steel wire						171	171
	Zippers and fasteners		200					200
	Subtotal							4 667
Group E:	*Service Companies*							
	Banking and finance		5	148		2	20	175
	Transportation			2			160	162
	Hotels			400				400
	Subtotal							737
	Total	1 230	1 174	4 274	399	372	5 970	13 419
	% of Total	9.2	8.7	31.9	3.0	2.8	44.4	100.0

Table 3-7: *Direct Effects of Japanese Companies: Select Data*

	Energy & Resource Companies	Merchandising Companies	Trading Companies	Manufacturing Companies	Service Companies	Total
Direct Employment:						
Employee Person-Years	3 390	4 029	596	4 667	737	13 419
Direct Wages and Salaries:						
Gross Wages & Salaries Paid ($ 000s)	57 780	50 903	7 530	99 896	9 570	225 679
Direct Value Added:						
Gross Domestic Product at Factor Cost ($ 000s)	165 479	67 772	10 026	130 841	13 452	387 570

million, mainly in resource activities (43 per cent) and manufacturing (34 per cent).

Analysis of the total (induced) impact of these companies' operations is presented in Chapter 4.

Notes

1. Statistics Canada, Business Finance Division, *Inter-Corporate Ownership: 1980.*

2. *Oriental Economist (Toyo Keizai Shinposha), Japanese Overseas Investment: A Complete Listing by Firms and Countries.*

3. Joan Gherson, "Japanese Investment in Canada."

4. Data supplied by Canadian Association of Japanese Automotive Dealers.

5. For a full study of the economic activity generated in Canada from the import of foreign-made autos, see Harbridge House, Inc., *The Imported Automobile Industry in Canada: An assessment of key aspects of its impact on the Canadian Economy and the Canadian Consumer.*

6. Yoshi Tsurumi with Rebecca R. Tsurumi, *Sogoshosha: Engines of Export-Based Growth.*

7. See Methodological Appendix for details.

4: Economic Impact

The previous chapter discussed and measured the *direct* economic effects of Japanese companies in Canada. The results presented were estimates of the value of labour and other factors of production demanded and consumed directly in the conduct of their business operations. The acquisition of these direct inputs stimulates, in turn, further production of goods and services as the employees and suppliers of the Japanese firms spend the incomes they have received. Thus the initial direct demand created by the Japanese companies induces additional, indirect production and value added throughout other sectors of the economy. The full economic impact of the Japanese companies is best represented as a combination of direct and induced effects, as presented below.

Using the patterns of direct demand from the previous chapter and taking account of the nature of the activities involved, Statistics Canada input-output models were used to simulate the economic impact of Japanese businesses in Canada. First, five simulations were run on the National Input-Output Model, one for each of the five main groups of Japanese firms listed in Chapter 3. The results provide estimates of the total employment and value-added impact for each of the groups, distributed among forty economic sectors. Secondly, combined data for the five groups of firms were used in a Provincial Input-Output Model simulation to estimate the distribution of employment and value-added impacts by province.

Several cautions are called for at this point. The first is that the input-output models used here are intended mainly for highly aggregated, macro-economic analysis. Simulations using small subsets, as in this study, are subject to substantial error. The results should be interpreted as general indicators of the magnitude and distribution of impacts, rather than as precise estimates. Secondly, the simulation results are based on average labour/output and other productivity

51

ratios of Canadian companies in each of the activities specified, assuming similar profiles for Japanese firms in Canada. This appears to
be a generally reasonable assumption. It is acknowledged, however,
that Japanese firms may be atypical in some respects, and for this
reason the relevance of the impact results may be reduced. Thirdly, it
should be recalled that the Japanese business presence has a variety of
other beneficial effects for Canada beyond those immediately quantified in the present analysis. These are discussed at length in Chapter 5.

Sectoral Impact

Table 4-1 presents estimates of the total employment impact of Japanese business in Canada, by economic sector, for each of the five major
company groups. The simulation results indicate that in 1981 some
39 700 jobs in Canada were associated directly or indirectly with the
Japanese business presence. Over 85 per cent of that total was generated by two of the company groups: manufacturing, including forest
products (45.5%), and services (39.9%). The employment benefits,
while spread widely, tend to accrue mainly in several sectors of Canada's economy. The greatest employment impact, by far, is in wholesale trade, where 6999 jobs are induced directly or indirectly by Japanese business activity. Significant employment is generated also in
retail trade (3810 jobs), agriculture (3742 jobs), and forestry (3730 jobs).

It would be incorrect to say that all of these 39 700 jobs are *created*
by Japanese business activity in Canada. Even without the Japanese,
some of the economic functions which they perform would surely
have been undertaken by Canadians or by other foreigners. It is reasonable to assert, however, that an estimated 39 700 jobs in Canada are
associated directly or indirectly with the Japanese business activity. It
is in that context that the figures in this section should be taken.

Simulation results indicating the total value added (gross domestic
product at factor cost) by Japanese business activity are shown as
Table 4-2. According to these projections, over $1.151 billion of Can-
ada's gross domestic product (GDP) was associated directly or indirectly with Japanese business activity in 1981. More than $100
million-worth of value was added in each of four economic sectors:
mineral fuels ($195 million), wholesale trade ($136 million), finance
($115 million), and forestry ($115 million).

Provincial Impact

Tables 4-3 and 4-4 present data on the provincial distribution of employment and value added. As the Provincial Model used in this sec-

Table 4-1: *Impact of Japanese Companies: Total Employment by Economic Sector^a (Man-Years)*

	Resource Companies	Merchand. Companies	Trading Companies	Manufact. Companies	Service Companies	All Companies
1. Agriculture	1 150.0	185.6	27.5	2 308.0	71.0	3 712.1
2. Forestry	21.0	10.3	1.5	3 694.8	2.1	3 729.7
3. Fishing, hunting & trapping	282.1	3.8	0.6	12.6	2.0	301.1
4. Metal mines	20.3	2.1	0.3	22.4	0.5	45.6
5. Mineral fuels	2 789.7	8.0	1.2	32.4	2.3	2 833.6
6. Non-metal mines & quarries	7.0	1.3	0.2	8.2	0.4	17.1
7. Services incidental to mining	206.1	2.0	0.3	9.8	0.6	218.1
8. Food & beverage industries	680.3	106.4	15.7	477.9	38.5	1 318.8
9. Tobacco-products industries	8.7	5.0	0.7	14.0	1.1	29.5
10. Rubber- & plastics-products industries	62.0	21.6	3.2	91.0	4.6	182.4
11. Leather industries	23.0	12.5	1.8	35.9	2.7	75.9
12. Textile industries	55.1	27.9	4.1	92.0	7.0	186.1
13. Knitting mills	20.1	11.3	1.7	32.3	2.4	67.8
14. Clothing industries	101.4	55.5	8.2	158.1	12.1	335.3
15. Wood industries	33.6	17.5	2.6	49.9	2.7	106.3
16. Furniture & fixture industries	32.5	18.4	2.7	62.9	4.0	120.5
17. Paper & allied industries	65.9	41.1	6.1	119.0	8.8	240.9
18. Printing & publishing	98.7	81.9	12.1	175.2	17.1	385.0
19. Primary metal industries	63.9	13.5	2.0	220.2	3.0	302.6
20. Metal-fabricating industries	94.6	27.7	4.1	167.4	5.7	299.5
21. Machinery industries	74.7	11.2	1.7	183.0	3.2	273.8
22. Transportation-equipment industries	48.3	15.1	2.2	65.4	9.7	140.7
23. Electrical products industries	67.2	20.8	3.1	1 496.8	5.1	1 593.0
24. Non-metallic mineral products industries	24.2	8.1	1.2	40.1	2.1	75.7
25. Petroleum & coal products industries	26.9	11.0	1.6	42.0	3.5	85.0
26. Chemical & chemical products industries	166.7	29.6	4.4	142.7	7.0	350.4
27. Miscellaneous manufacturing industries	50.1	25.4	3.8	301.1	5.6	386.0
28. Construction industry	200.3	64.0	9.5	270.0	17.0	560.8
29. Transportation & storage	498.4	261.2	38.6	1 317.4	236.7	2 352.3
30. Communication	236.1	200.5	29.7	394.2	38.5	899.0

Table 4-1 continued

	Resource Companies	Merchand. Companies	Trading Companies	Manufact. Companies	Service Companies	All Companies
31. Electric power, gas, other utilities	148.9	55.1	8.1	186.2	13.1	411.4
32. Wholesale trade	765.1	4 463.2	660.3	1 050.1	59.9	6 998.6
33. Retail trade	1 131.5	580.8	85.9	1 880.9	130.7	3 809.8
34. Owner-occupied dwellings	0.0	0.0	0.0	0.0	0.0	0.0
35. Other finance, insurance, & real estate	743.6	318.9	47.2	825.6	245.7	2 181.0
36. Education & health insurance	63.4	36.1	5.3	100.5	7.8	213.1
37. Amusement & recreation services	75.7	46.2	6.8	122.9	11.6	263.2
38. Services to business management	496.3	290.4	43.0	671.9	59.7	1 561.3
39. Accommodation & food services	535.9	345.8	51.2	855.7	512.4	2 301.0
40. Other personal & miscellaneous services	203.9	110.7	16.4	343.5	27.7	702.2
Total	11 373.2	7 547.5	1 116.6	18 073.0	1 585.6	39 696.9
Per cent of total	28.7	19.0	2.8	45.5	39.9	100.0

Note
a. From Statistics Canada National Input-Output Model simulation, using 1981 data.

Table 4-2: *Impact of Japanese Companies: Gross Domestic Product at Factor Cost, by Economic Sector* [a] *($ 000s)*

	Resource Companies	Merchand. Companies	Trading Companies	Manufact. Companies	Service Companies	All Companies
1. Agriculture	20 453	3 300	488	41 046	1 262	66 549
2. Forestry	644	316	47	113 516	65	114 588
3. Fishing hunting & trapping	6 739	91	13	301	47	7 191
4. Metal mines	1 105	132	19	1 348	31	2 635
5. Mineral fuels	181 751	2 394	354	9 326	712	194 537
6. Non-metal mines & quarries	463	82	12	542	25	1 124
7. Services incidental to mining	6 805	65	10	323	19	7 222
8. Food & beverage industries	17 797	3 743	553	21 078	1 308	44 479
9. Tobacco-products industries	389	224	34	618	48	1 313
10. Rubber- & plastics-products industries	1 697	586	86	2 491	125	4 985
11. Leather industries	390	212	31	611	46	1 290
12. Textile industries	1 292	653	96	2 144	164	4 349
13. Knitting mills	370	208	31	595	44	1 248
14. Clothing industries	1 784	977	144	2 782	212	5 899
15. Wood industries	955	470	70	1 393	77	2 965
16. Furniture & fixture industries	660	373	55	1 294	82	2 464
17. Paper & allied industries	2 533	1 589	235	4 518	340	9 215
18. Printing & publishing	2 686	2 226	329	4 765	464	10 470
19. Primary metal industries	2 480	521	77	8 222	118	11 418
20. Metal-fabricating industries	3 518	997	147	13 636	208	18 506
21. Machinery industries	2 314	335	49	5 708	96	8 502
22. Transportation-equipment industries	1 630	476	71	2 102	282	4 561
23. Electrical products industries	2 033	634	94	43 777	156	46 694
24. Non-metallic mineral products industries	860	278	41	1 381	72	2 632
25. Petroleum & coal-products industries	1 298	529	78	2 026	169	4 100
26. Chemical & chemical products industries	6 300	1 166	173	5 704	277	13 620
27. Miscellaneous manufacturing industries	1 157	589	88	6 588	131	8 553
28. Construction industry	6 158	2 072	307	8 369	541	17 447
29. Transportation & storage	12 463	6 355	940	32 108	6 416	58 282

Table 4-2 continued

	Resource Companies	Merchand. Companies	Trading Companies	Manufact. Companies	Service Companies	All Companies
30. Communication	7 519	6 127	906	12 464	1 230	28 246
31. Electric power, gas, other utilities	9 061	3 370	498	11 434	799	25 162
32. Wholesale trade	14 855	86 653	12 818	20 388	1 162	135 876
33. Retail trade	18 974	9 740	1 441	31 540	2 191	63 886
34. Owner-occupied dwellings	9 044	5 182	767	14 443	1 108	30 544
35. Other finance, insurance & real estate	40 741	14 186	2 099	49 324	8 780	115 130
36. Education & health insurance	1 780	1 012	150	2 819	218	5 979
37. Amusement & recreation services	1 612	974	144	2 608	250	5 588
38. Services to business management	7 879	4 535	671	10 483	929	24 497
39. Accommodation & food services	7 270	4 691	694	11 609	6 952	31 216
40. Other personal & miscellaneous services	2 413	1 288	191	4 100	326	8 318
Total	409 872	169 351	25 051	509 524	37 482	1 151 280
Per cent of total	35.6	14.7	2.2	44.3	3.3	100.0

Notes
a. From statistics Canada National Input-Output Model simulation, using 1981 data.

tion is run independently of the National Model of the preceeding
section, simulation results differ slightly at the aggregate national
level, despite identical inputs.

According to the Provincial Model employment-simulation results
(Table 4-3), a total of 36 408 jobs across Canada were associated with
the Japanese presence in 1981. The employment benefits accrued most
heavily to two provinces: British Columbia, where Japanese businesses provided 13 442 jobs or 36.9 per cent of the national total, and
Ontario, where they provided 12 142 jobs or 33.3 per cent of the national total. Quebec ranks a distant third, with Japanese businesses
providing 4815 jobs or 13.2 per cent of the national total. Jobs provided by Japanese businesses in the prairie provinces of Manitoba,
Saskatchewan and Alberta together account for only 9.7 per cent of the
national total; the remaining 6.7 per cent are provided in the Maritimes, mainly in New Brunswick.

Table 4-4 shows total value added (GDP at factor cost), by province.
According to the Provincial Model simulation, $1.260 billion of Can-
ada's 1981 GDP was generated directly or indirectly by Japanese companies. Most striking is the very high proportion (47.6%) of the national total generated in British Columbia. Slightly over 25 per cent
was generated in Ontario; 10.2 per cent in Alberta; 9.5 per cent in
Quebec; and 7.6 per cent in all of the remaining provinces combined.

Summary

The simulation results indicate that some 36 000-40 000 jobs in Canada are associated with Japanese business activity, as is some $1.2
billion of GDP. These numbers may seem small in proportion to the
overall economy. The total employment associated with Japanese business, for example, represents only one-third of 1 per cent of the Canadian labour force. But the effects are significant. In the recent reces-
sionary environment, while governments in Canada have been
expending enormous financial resources in attempts to create jobs and
stimulate domestic production, Japanese companies are generating
thousands of jobs and more than $1 billion of annual domestic output
at virtually no direct cost to the Canadian taxpayer. This is not to say
that the benefits are free of cost: there are, of course, associated outflows of natural resources and dividends, and there is some surrender
of domestic economic control. But the nature of Japanese investment,
described in Chapter 2, is such that the financial costs and loss of
control are minimal.

The geographic distribution of the benefits derived from the Japanese business activity is also highly significant. As expected, the simu-

Table 4-3: *Impact of Japanese Companies: Total Employment, by Province[a] (Man-Years)*

	Nfld.	PEI	NS	NB	Que.	Ont.	Man.	Sask.	Alta.	BC	Y+NWT	Canada
1. Agriculture	0.1	3.5	4.6	15.6	31.5	102.3	15.2	32.0	344.9	113.4	0.0	663.0
2. Forestry	0.6	0.0	0.8	1 498.5	24.2	18.2	2.8	0.6	2.5	2 099.1	0.0	3 647.2
3. Fishing, hunting & trapping	0.2	0.1	4.3	2.2	0.6	0.1	0.1	0.0	0.0	144.2	0.0	151.9
4. Metal mines	0.1	0.0	0.0	0.9	13.4	20.0	3.0	2.3	0.0	3.6	0.8	44.2
5. Mineral fuels	0.0	0.0	3.7	0.8	0.0	0.0	0.2	1.4	63.3	2 707.0	0.0	2 776.4
6. Non-metal mines & quarries	0.2	0.0	0.4	0.5	1.6	3.2	0.2	6.9	1.0	4.0	0.0	18.0
7. Services incidental to mining	0.0	0.0	0.0	0.2	0.7	1.0	0.6	0.8	13.6	28.4	0.1	45.3
8. Food & beverage industries	1.7	3.0	20.3	33.3	124.1	268.9	32.3	14.0	279.2	656.3	0.0	1 433.1
9. Tobacco-products industries	0.0	0.0	0.0	0.0	19.0	10.3	0.0	0.0	0.0	0.0	0.0	29.3
10. Rubber- & plastics-products industries	0.0	0.0	2.3	0.5	41.1	113.9	0.9	0.2	12.4	15.9	0.0	187.1
11. Leather industries	0.1	0.0	0.0	1.7	37.5	40.9	2.3	0.0	0.9	3.3	0.0	86.7
12. Textile industries	0.0	0.2	3.2	0.8	112.2	89.9	3.7	0.7	2.6	22.2	0.0	235.4
13. Knitting mills	0.0	0.0	5.0	0.0	49.9	27.9	1.2	0.0	0.6	3.1	0.0	87.7
14. Clothing industries	0.0	0.0	0.4	0.9	210.5	75.9	22.0	3.5	9.9	18.3	0.0	341.5
15. Wood industries	0.1	0.0	1.2	3.9	24.0	31.1	3.0	0.8	5.7	59.6	0.0	129.4
16. Furniture & fixture industries	0.0	0.0	0.6	1.6	44.7	66.8	6.7	0.6	7.0	22.2	0.0	150.1
17. Paper & allied industries	0.9	0.0	4.1	3.9	84.1	142.7	10.9	0.8	9.8	63.2	0.0	320.4
18. Printing & publishing	0.1	0.2	1.3	8.2	81.0	221.4	16.7	2.7	22.4	116.2	0.0	470.1
19. Primary metal industries	0.0	0.0	5.0	2.2	61.5	166.6	6.0	0.8	14.2	60.1	0.0	316.5
20. Metal-fabricating industries	0.0	0.1	0.5	4.3	73.8	213.8	10.9	2.0	13.9	297.6	0.0	617.0
21. Machinery industries	0.0	0.0	0.1	1.6	35.8	194.7	3.8	0.9	8.3	116.2	0.0	361.6
22. Transportation-equipment industries	0.0	0.1	3.3	4.2	25.3	84.5	7.4	0.7	7.1	51.6	0.0	184.4
23. Electrical products industries	0.0	0.0	1.8	3.5	503.2	1 101.4	4.8	0.3	4.1	20.9	0.0	1 640.0

Table 4-3 continued

	Nfld.	PEI	NS	NB	Que.	Ont.	Man.	Sask.	Alta.	BC	Y+NWT	Canada
24. Non-metallic mineral products industries	0.0	0.0	0.3	1.9	14.1	39.4	0.9	0.4	18.1	33.1	0.0	108.1
25. Petroleum & coal products industries	0.7	0.0	0.7	2.0	6.3	34.2	0.9	1.1	13.3	23.4	0.0	82.6
26. Chemical & chemical prod. industries	0.3	0.2	0.8	1.1	92.6	199.6	3.1	0.7	40.0	146.1	0.0	484.4
27. Misc. manufacturing industries	0.0	0.0	0.2	5.6	251.7	114.8	2.9	0.6	4.7	33.2	0.0	413.7
28. Construction industry	0.4	0.3	2.8	33.2	53.9	131.9	10.6	5.9	69.0	181.5	0.0	489.7
29. Transportation & storage	1.2	1.4	16.2	91.9	328.8	644.8	40.4	17.9	167.8	797.3	0.0	2 107.8
30. Communication	0.4	0.4	7.4	34.5	161.9	342.9	28.6	8.7	88.5	309.3	0.0	982.6
31. Electric power, gas, other utilities	2.0	0.2	1.7	12.1	37.6	107.7	8.8	4.8	48.7	217.9	0.0	441.5
32. Wholesale trade	1.5	1.6	19.9	81.1	992.1	3 711.3	442.7	22.4	249.7	1 422.5	0.0	6 944.7
33. Retail trade	1.3	1.5	13.2	219.3	362.7	1 019.3	88.2	35.4	350.5	1 513.8	0.1	3 605.2
34. Other finance, insurance & real estate	0.7	0.6	13.1	28.2	359.0	969.3	46.0	17.5	151.9	425.2	0.0	2 011.5
35. Education & health insurance	0.0	0.0	0.5	8.6	21.5	65.0	5.9	2.2	12.8	62.9	0.0	179.4
36. Amusement & recreation services	0.0	0.1	0.7	6.2	32.7	99.4	7.3	1.5	17.2	83.1	0.0	248.1
37. Services to business management	0.5	0.5	10.1	59.8	273.4	661.3	29.0	11.4	109.6	527.6	0.0	1 683.2
38. Accommodation & food services	0.5	0.7	6.3	77.4	177.4	869.1	50.7	16.9	173.9	854.5	0.2	2 227.6
39. Other personal & misc. services	0.1	0.2	1.8	29.3	49.9	136.7	11.2	6.3	41.5	184.3	0.0	461.3
Total	13.8	14.6	158.6	2 281.3	4 815.2	12 142.5	931.9	226.0	2 380.7	13 441.8	1.5	36 407.9
Per cent of total	0.0	0.0	0.4	6.3	13.2	33.3	2.6	0.6	6.5	36.9	0.0	100.0

Note
a. From Statistics Canada Provincial Input-Output Model simulation, using 1981 data.

Table 4-4: Impact of Japanese Companies: Gross Domestic Product at Factor Cost, by Province[a] ($ 000s)

	Nfld.	PEI	NS	NB	Que.	Ont.	Man.	Sask.	Alta.	BC	Y+NWT	Canada
1. Agriculture	2	150	136	393	1729	6295	1812	8116	48336	4007	0	70975
2. Forestry	10	0	15	30228	506	376	33	12	30	79223	0	110433
3. Fishing, hunting & trapping	10	7	177	47	30	13	5	6	12	10345	0	10651
4. Metal mines	6	0	0	46	567	1359	163	117	0	276	110	2645
5. Mineral fuels	0	0	23	58	0	12	69	509	14460	243720	0	258852
6. Non-metal mines & quarries	7	0	16	21	84	173	9	746	68	182	0	1305
7. Services incidental to mining	1	0	1	4	23	35	18	23	556	979	3	1643
8. Food & beverage industries	21	44	341	860	3123	7488	697	392	9436	23553	0	45955
9. Tobacco-products industries	0	0	0	0	672	591	0	0	0	0	0	1262
10. Rubber & plastics-products industries	0	0	27	11	844	2827	19	6	243	380	0	4456
11. Leather industries	2	0	0	11	522	560	41	0	15	54	0	1204
12. Textile industries	0	3	43	8	2146	1969	50	31	53	351	0	4654
13. Knitting mills	0	0	64	6	793	372	23	0	10	42	0	1310
14. Clothing industries	0	0	3	8	2908	1108	273	43	169	266	0	4778
15. Wood industries	1	0	20	73	532	657	53	23	119	1435	0	2913
16. Furniture & fixture industries	0	0	7	20	736	1102	98	5	116	369	0	2452
17. Paper & allied industries	34	0	121	191	2910	4545	407	41	290	2884	0	11423
18. Printing & publishing	2	3	28	149	2033	5028	365	55	562	2529	0	10753
19. Primary metal industries	0	0	75	44	1487	5550	197	22	473	1653	0	9501
20. Metal-fabricating industries	0	0	15	97	1952	5623	285	50	471	10669	0	19164
21. Machinery industries	0	0	1	32	832	4860	77	21	204	2964	0	8991
22. Transportation-equipment industries	1	1	38	64	477	2762	199	11	151	1338	0	5042
23. Electrical products industries	0	0	45	66	12068	28633	104	5	74	450	0	41445
24. Non-metallic mineral products industries	1	0	7	51	393	1210	23	11	697	954	0	3347
25. Petroleum & coal-products industries	26	0	179	105	719	994	99	49	562	1689	0	4423
26. Chemical & chemical-products												

Table 4-4 continued

	Nfld.	PEI	NS	NB	Que.	Ont.	Man.	Sask.	Alta.	BC	Y+NWT	Canada
industries	8	5	16	45	2 668	7 167	107	24	1 731	4 517	0	16 289
27. Misc. manufacturing industries	0	0	3	93	3 903	2 364	46	8	80	604	0	7 101
28. Construction industry	11	8	74	965	1 577	3 903	286	222	2 239	6 891	2	16 177
29. Transportation & storage	43	57	440	2 436	9 875	19 821	1 105	549	4 561	19 877	0	58 765
30. Communication	10	9	143	839	4 160	9 518	653	235	2 420	8 152	1	26 139
31. Electric power, gas, other utilities	232	7	56	480	2 195	5 088	475	253	2 946	10 606	1	22 338
32. Wholesale trade	28	30	405	1 439	23 966	87 971	10 620	612	7 164	39 901	0	172 136
33. Retail trade	20	28	233	3 491	6 404	15 916	1 356	697	6 339	27 583	2	62 070
34. Owner occupied dwellings	8	10	108	1 216	1 812	9 212	614	317	3 013	13 381	1	29 693
35. Other finance, insurance & real estate	19	18	449	6 032	12 470	34 962	1 581	1 169	11 452	44 142	3	112 297
36. Education & health insurance	1	2	20	288	784	2 315	167	72	669	2 946	0	7 265
37. Amusement & recreation services	1	2	14	191	606	1 768	103	31	389	1 776	0	4 880
38. Services to business management	9	9	173	720	5 164	11 820	599	236	2 469	8 627	0	29 826
39. Accommodation & food services	6	8	68	766	2 593	11 373	636	255	2 694	10 830	3	29 232
40. Other personal & misc. services	2	2	24	325	844	2 086	166	102	780	2 947	1	7 281
41. Households	6	7	84	1 081	1 977	6 258	512	251	2 046	6 710	0	18 933
Total	526	413	3 692	53 001	119 083	315 783	24 142	15 331	128 099	599 803	128	1 260 000
Per cent of total	0.0	0.0	0.3	4.2	9.5	25.1	1.9	1.2	10.2	47.6	0.0	100.0

Note
a. From Statistics Canada Provincial Input-Output Model simulation, using 1981 data.

lation results show total value added to be highest in Western Canada, especially in British Columbia, where 60 per cent of the national total is generated. But the employment benefits are spread much more widely: 53 per cent is generated in Eastern Canada, mainly in Ontario and Quebec, and 47 per cent in the Prairies and Western provinces, chiefly British Columbia. Thus, while the immediate impact of Japanese business activity in Canada appears to be highly concentrated, the derived benefits are distributed much more evenly across the country.

The widespread distribution of benefits revealed in this analysis is a highly significant feature of Japanese business in Canada. It is, in the author's opinion, a feature which is insufficiently recognized by Canadians, who tend to focus only on the more visible (and more highly concentrated) immediate effects.

5: Intangible Effects

The previous chapters of this study have measured and classified the specific demand, both immediate and induced, which Japanese business firms create in Canada. But the Japanese business presence has other far-reaching influences which are less direct and more difficult to quantify. This chapter discusses briefly some of these intangible effects. Considered in turn are the role of Japanese trading companies, the function of banks, project financing, purchase agreements, and technology and management transfer.

Trading Companies

The direct economic impact of the Japanese trading companies, measured narrowly in terms of their direct employment and consumption of goods and services, was discussed in Chapter 3. But the full economic importance of the trading companies extends far more widely. With their ample financial resources and their vast global information and communications networks, they play a key role in generating trade and stimulating investments in Canada.[1]

About 65 per cent of the volume of trading companies involves exports to Japan, mainly coking coal, copper, nickel, wheat, rapeseed oil, pulp, wood and chemicals. Twenty-six per cent consists of imports from Japan, including steel, industrial machinery, TV tubes, and mineral fuels. The remaining 9 per cent of their volume is accounted for by trade between Canada and countries other than Japan.

Table 5-1 summarizes the trade activity in 1980 of the nine general trading companies in Canada. Together, these companies handled nearly $5 *billion* worth of Canadian trade, accounting for 71 per cent of all Canadian exports to Japan and 41 per cent of Canada's imports from Japan. In addition to their bilateral activities, the trading companies have begun to play an increasingly important role in Canadian trade with other countries. They exported $256 million-worth of Canadian products to third countries in 1980, including major shipments of rapeseed oil to India, Australia and Africa, and made sales of fertilizers and chemicals to a variety of countries. In the same year, they handled $156 million-worth of third-country imports into Canada.

The trading companies also play an extremely important role in generating Japanese investment in Canada. The nine general trading companies had invested the equivalent of US$179 million in Canada as of 1981 (see Table 5-2), that is, about one-third of all Japanese investment in Canada. Moreover, in addition to maintaining their own investment positions, the trading companies have served as the key promoters and catalysts in drawing investments by other Japanese companies to Canada, through joint ventures. Their impact thus extends well beyond their own immediate investment positions.

Banks

Japanese banks have played a minor role in Canada in terms of direct employment and purchases, but an important intangible role behind the scenes. Prior to 1981, Canadian bank legislation restricted foreign banking presence in Canada to representative offices, which could neither accept deposits nor make loans. Under these rules, twelve Japanese banks established representative offices, all of them in Toronto: two long-term-credit banks, specializing in medium- and long-term credit, and ten 'city banks' similar to the major Canadian and American commercial banks. The typical Canadian representative office consisted of two or three Japanese bankers and a small, local, administrative staff.

Despite their inability to conduct direct commercial banking functions, these representative offices have performed a variety of services; they:

- Provide information on Japan to Canadian exporters and investors
- Gather information on Canada for Japanese exporters and investors
- Provide information about services which the Japanese parent bank could provide in Japan and the United States to prospective customers
- Refer potential loan business to United States branches of the Japanese banks, which could put loans on their books

Table 5-1: *Canadian Trade Handled by Nine Japanese General Trading Companies*[a]

Fiscal Year 1980[b]

	Imports Into Canada			Exports From Canada			General Trade
	From Japan	*From Other Countries*	*Total*	*To Japan*	*To Other Countries*	*Total*	
Trade volume ($ millions)	1 280	156	1 437	3 243	256	3 518	4 955
% of Total Trading-company volume	26%	3%	29%	65%	6%	71%	100%

Notes
a. Source: Consul General of Japan.
b. Fiscal Year 1980: 1 April 1980-31 March 1981

Table 5-2: *Investment in Canada by Nine Japanese General Trading Companies*[a] *in Fiscal Year 1981*[b]

	Investment by Japanese Parent			Investment by Canadian Subsidiary		
	Number of Projects	*Amount Invested US $000*	*Per cent of Total*	*Number of Projects*	*Amount Invested US $000*	*Per cent Total*
Resources	20	40 210	22.5	2	800	18.3
Manufacturing	14	53 650	30.0	7	2 490	56.8
Distribution & Sales	22	84 970	47.5	5	1 090	24.9
Total	56	178 830	100.0	14	4 380	100.0

Notes
a. Source: Consul General of Japan.
b. Fiscal Year 1981: 1 April 1981-31 March 1982.

- 'Show the flag' for Japanese banks seeking world-wide status
- Deal with Canadian banks on matters affecting correspondent relationships.

Revisions of the Canadian Bank Act, effective January 1981, have set the stage for a more direct and substantial involvement of Japanese banks in Canada.[2] Under the new terms, a limited number of foreign banks are permitted to open full-service branches in Canada, subject to two important constraints:

- Total assets of all foreign banks are limited to 8 per cent of the total domestic assets of all banks in Canada.
- Each foreign bank must limit its assets in Canada to twenty times its deemed capital base.

The first Japanese bank to be granted a charter for full banking operations in Canada was Bank of Tokyo, by virtue of its being represented longest in Canada, that is, for over twenty years. Bank of Tokyo Canada has its headquarters in Toronto, with branches in Vancouver and Calgary. As of December 1983, six other Japanese banks—Dai-Ichi Kangyo Bank, Fuji Bank, Industrial Bank of Japan, Mitsui Bank, Mitsubishi Bank, and Sanwa Bank—had been granted charters to establish branches in Canada. (See Table 3-9 for the current status of each of the banks.)

The emphasis of the Japanese banks, once they have assumed full operations in Canada, will fall almost entirely on wholesale commercial banking. None of these banks is expected to engage in significant retail banking. The Industrial Bank of Japan will continue to stress lending to federal and provincial governments and financing major resource projects, as it previously did from Tokyo. The Bank of Tokyo, Fuji Bank, and Mitsui Bank are likely to maintain their special emphasis on project financing and foreign exchange dealings. The other city banks will offer general wholesale commercial services, directed largely at companies involved in Canadian-Japanese trade.[3]

Project Financing

Chapter 3 emphasized that the direct impact of Japanese involvement in Canada's resources sectors is small: equity participation of Japanese firms is insignificant, and their direct employment is limited generally to a handful of liaison officers and technical advisers. Nevertheless, the Japanese play an exceedingly important indirect role in providing loan financing and purchase contracts essential to the viability of some of Canada's most ambitious mega-projects. While the full impact of such indirect participation cannot be measured precisely, it constitutes probably the most substantial and far-reaching benefit to Canadians of any facet of the Japanese business presence.

The function and importance of Japanese financing and purchase contracts vary with the type of resource. This section will focus on the nature and size of Japanese loans to Canadian petroleum projects. The following section will discuss the function of Japanese financing and purchase contracts in coal development, which is substantially different.

Japanese firms are discouraged by Canada's National Energy Policy (NEP) from participating directly in major petroleum projects. They are also precluded by the NEP from exporting Canadian oil or gas until such time as Canada achieves self-sufficiency in those products. Nevertheless, it is in Japan's interest to assist Canadians to explore and develop potential new oil and gas sources: if Canada produces more than enough oil and gas to satisfy its domestic needs, then both Canadians and Japanese can gain by exporting some of the surplus to Japan. Even if oil export is not permitted, new oil discoveries in Canada would tend to reduce pressure in the world market, thus benefiting Japan. With this end in mind, the Japanese have committed large amounts of loan financing to Canadian petroleum projects in the Arctic and in Alberta tar sands. In doing so without any assurance of the projects' success or of governmental approval to export oil even if they are successful, the Japanese are also sharing significantly in the risk these projects involve.[4]

Because of the large investments and high risks involved, the Japanese financing is done through consortia. In the case of Arctic oil exploration in the Beaufort Sea, a group of forty-four Japanese companies joined together with the government-owned Japan National Oil Company (JANOC) to form Arctic Petroleum Corporation (APC) in February 1981. The Japanese participants include trading companies, shipbuilding companies, oil refineries, and oil-exploration companies. Through the window of APC, the Japanese have agreed to provide more than $400 million in exploration loans to Dome Petroleum Company, the Canadian principal: $200 million to be paid out in 1982, and $100 million in each of 1983 and 1984. Pending the outcome of the current feasibility studies and approval by the National Energy Board, the Japanese participants are expected to contribute an additional $800 million in development loans, or approximately 20 per cent of the total project financing. The loans are provided at extremely favourable rates of interest (4-6%) and without guarantee of repayment. Under the most optimistic outcome, APC will be repaid in oil, for export to Japan. If Canada's National Energy Board does not permit export, APC will be paid in oil to sell domestically for dollars which it could then use to purchase oil elsewhere. However, no such export or 'swap' arrangements will be permitted until Canada has achieved a domestic oil surplus. If the projects prove non-viable, or if Canada fails to achieve oil self-sufficiency, the Japanese would recover their loan principal, but would earn no interest on capital which, by that time, may have been tied up for years. In addition to its loan financing, APC has donated $15 million as an outright grant to Dome's Arctic Exploration Research Program.

Similar financial arrangements underlie Japan's participation in two major Alberta oil-sands projects. The Japanese are providing money in return for a possible share of the output. If the output is not large enough to permit export of the product, they will recover only their loan principal, without interest or other earnings. The Japan Petroleum Association and sixty-seven private Japanese companies began their participation at Athabasca in 1978. Japanese loans are expected to total $7.48 million over fifteen years, or 25 per cent of the total financing. In the Primrose/Cold Lake project, a consortium of Japanese companies has committed some $12.8 million to exploration and feasibility studies.

It was not imperative that the Arctic and oil-sands financing come from Japan. Funds could have been raised in other world financial centres. But the Japanese were willing to supply the funds at lower cost and to absorb a greater share of risk, partly because of special insurance coverage provided by the Japanese government. Moreover, Canadian executives interviewed in the present study emphasized a preference for Japanese participation in their enterprises because the Japanese are considered reliable partners, and because of possibilities they offer for subsequent co-operation in other energy-related projects.

Purchase Agreements

The petroleum projects discussed above involved Japanese financial support, but not purchase contracts. In dealing with oil, the relevant question is not whether the Japanese will buy, but whether the Canadians will sell. This is because Canada is not yet self-sufficient in oil, and it could easily find other buyers if it were. The situation with coal is different. Canada is able to produce much more metallurgical coal than it can use domestically, and it can do so for many decades into the future without exhausting known reserves. But the large capital investments required to exploit these surplus deposits cannot be made without firm guarantees of sustained demand. While some demand for Canadian coal exists in smaller Asian and Latin American countries, by far the largest potential export market is Japan.

Japanese participation has been essential to a number of existing coal-mining operations, mostly in southern British Columbia. In several of these projects, Japanese companies hold minority equity positions, and in others they provide loans. But common to all the projects is the existence of long-term purchase contracts, often running up to fifteen years' duration, for the sale of their output to Japanese firms. It is the purchase contracts, more than the actual financing provided, which ensure the viability of the mining projects.

The most dramatic example of the beneficial impact of Japanese purchase agreements is a project under way, but not yet completed: the North East Coal Development, the largest industrial undertaking in British Columbia's history and the largest mining development ever in Canada. The focal organization is Quintette Coal Ltd., in which Japanese trading companies, mining companies, and ten Japanese steel mills, together, own 38 per cent of the equity. Quintette announced on 30 June 1982 that it had arranged financing of $1.3 billion to develop a coal mine in northeast British Columbia.[5] A consortium of seven banks (four Japanese, two Canadian, and one French) have agreed to underwrite up to $950 million in long-term debt. The balance of the funds will be provided by equity from Quintette's shareholders. Another, smaller mine will be developed at nearby Bull-moose, BC, by Tech Corporation.

The North East Coal Development is a massive project comparable to the James Bay power project, the Syncrude project, and the Alaska Highway pipeline. In addition to the development of the mines, it will involve the construction of new towns, railways, highways, power lines, and a deep-sea terminal at Prince Rupert, BC. The project is expected to result in the creation of 10 600 permanent jobs, 5700 of them in Western Canada and 4900 in the East. According to one consultant's study, Ottawa stands to receive $1.6 billion in revenue from the development over fifteen years, while Victoria will gain $350 million.[6] But this entire massive project was contingent upon a long-term sales contract signed with a consortium of Japanese steel mills in January 1981. Under the terms of the contract, Quintette Coal Ltd. will deliver five million metric tonnes of metallurgical coal to Japan each year for fifteen years, starting in the fall of 1983. The price is set at $75.50 per metric tonne in 1980 dollars, and is subject to increases based on a complex indexing formula adjusting for inflation. Quintette has also announced a new contract for 1.3 million metric tonnes of thermal coal a year for fifteen years, but extendable for another five years; this new contract is worth nearly $1.4 billion. It is clear that without these and related purchase contracts with the Japanese, neither the Japanese financing nor the domestic funding for this important project could have been raised, as the only market of sufficient size is Japan.[7]

Japanese purchase contracts have also played a very important role in the development of the Canadian uranium industry. Although Japanese companies have not participated directly in uranium exploration and mining companies, as have the Europeans, Japan has been a major purchaser of uranium from Canadian producers, particularly in the mid-1970s, when enormous quantities of Canadian uranium were purchased by Japanese utilities. Some of the purchase contracts represented up to ten years of total production capabilities of the Canadian suppliers.

Technology and Management Transfer

An often-cited potential benefit of the Japanese business presence in Canada is technology transfer: Canadians may acquire valuable new technology through the Japanese investments or by licensing agreements with Japanese firms. Experts interviewed in the present research point to several instances of successful technology transfer. As examples, a Japanese-developed hydraulic coal-mining process is now employed in the British Columbia coal fields; and Alcan Aluminium Company is introducing in its Canadian smelters a new electrolytic pot under license from Sumitomo Company of Japan. But aside from a small handful of such examples, the research suggests that to date, Canada has received very little in the way of technology transfer from Japan. This probably is not surprising, as the focus of Japanese attention in Canada is on the extraction and processing of natural resources, activities in which Japan has only limited first-hand experience. It is likely that Japanese technology inputs will be more substantial in some of the high-technology resource-based projects, such as the production of liquified natural gas and the construction of petrochemical complexes, which are planned for the future.

Despite the world-wide attention given to supposedly superior management techniques, the Japanese business presence in Canada seems to have had negligible influence on management practices. The management of most Japanese business affiliates in Canada appears remarkably similar to that of comparable Canadian-owned businesses. One reason is that the effects of Japanese management practices are most visible in manufacturing operations, but the amount of Japanese manufacturing investment in Canada is insignificant. Japanese managers interviewed in the present research also cite Canadian labour unions as a major obstacle to their attempts to transfer management methods. Based on open, direct communication between management and workers, and on a feeling of mutually-shared values, the traditional Japanese management practices may be largely unworkable in Canada, given the militancy and perceived rigidity of the unions.

Notes

1. Yoshi Tsurumi with Rebecca R. Tsurumi, *Sogoshosha: Engines of Export-Based Growth.*

2. See, for example: "Here come the foreign banks," *Financial Times,* 14 September 1981, p. 23; "Foreign Banks: Opening doors under new rules," *Gazette* (Montreal), 3 October 1981, p. 93; "The revolution that never was?" *Financial Times,* 9 November 1981, p. 13; "New Act helps to enhance Canadian banks' role," *Globe and Mail* (Toronto), 14 December 1981, p. B32; and "Backing of parent bank key to foreign units' survival," *Globe and Mail,* 15 February 1982, p. B33.

3. Negotiations have been announced for Japanese commercial banks to fund up to $11 billion in loans to Canada for construction of planned pipelines to carry natural gas from Alaska to the US mainland, "Pipeline firms look to Japan for funding," *Globe and Mail,* 27 January 1982, p. B5.

4. "Oil self-sufficiency no sure thing," *Financial Post,* 12 June 1982, p. 9.

5. "Banks to finance new coal projects," *Province* (Vancouver), 30 June 1982, p. 1; "Japanese 'won't control price of coal': Quinette mine financing in place," *Sun* (Vancouver), 30 June 1982, p. D5.

6. "A Project that stays," *Globe and Mail,* 3 July 1982, p. 8.

7. "Japanese Concept Saves Northeast B.C. Coal Deal," *Sun,* 3 July 1982, p. A1.

6: A Look to the Future

On the surface, at least, Canada and Japan complement each other economically to an extraordinary degree: the former is sparsely settled, abundant in energy and resources, and lacking adequate domestic capital; the latter is densely populated, vastly short of energy and raw materials, and relatively abundant in capital. The mutual benefits from expanded business and economic interaction are enormous. Yet despite the substantial activity described in earlier chapters, Canadian-Japanese business activity remains small. Its full potential has hardly begun to be realized.

Opportunities

The main prospects for further Japanese business involvement in Canada lie overwhelmingly in the energy and resource areas. Canadians have placed high priority on massive megaprojects designed to develop new, untapped energy sources and to promote a major upgrading in the processing of existing resources. Japanese capital, skills, and markets can play a key role in many of these developments.

Chapter 5 discussed the important role of Japanese companies in major new oil-exploration and coal-mining developments already under way. Still other co-operative ventures lie further ahead. The most significant in its promise of far-reaching benefit to Canadians is the planned liquified natural gas (LNG) project. On 15 July 1982, the government of British Columbia announced approval of a plan submitted by Dome Petroleum with Nissho-Iwai Trading Company and a consortium of other Japanese firms, for a massive project to transfer, liquify and export surplus Canadian natural gas from Alberta through British Columbia to Japan.[1] Under the plan announced,

Dome will borrow more than $2 billion at 9 3/4 per cent from the Japanese participants over the next two decades, on the basis of advance purchase contracts already signed with Japanese buyers. The project is expected ultimately to involve $3 billion: roughly $1 billion to construct a pipeline from Alberta across British Columbia; $1 billion to build a liquification plant on the British Columbia coast; and $1 billion for the construction of transport vessels, possibly in Maritime shipyards. While the immediate focus of the project is on Alberta and British Columbia, the demand for pipeline, vessels and other capital goods would distribute economic gains across Canada. Also under discussion are plans for joint Canadian-Japanese efforts towards future construction of major petrochemical and fertilizer complexes, which could move Canadians substantially closer to their long-term objective of upgrading the manufactured content and value added of their resource-based industries.[2] A compendium of actual and potential resource-related projects in which major Japanese participation is likely is presented as Table 6-1.

Opportunities for greater Japanese business activity outside of the resource sectors are modest by comparison. The general trading companies will almost certainly retain an important role in both trade and investment. Some observers expect these companies to become increasingly active in promoting Canadian trade with third countries, other than Japan. In the merchandising sector, additional investments are likely to be made, but most of the major Japanese producers are already represented. Japanese manufacturing of end products in Canada, other than those related directly to resource projects, is likely to remain insignificant for the foreseeable future.

Obstacles

While the potential opportunities for additional Japanese investment in Canada are numerous, the obstacles to their realization are formidable. Interviews by the author with Japanese managers who have invested, or are considering investing, in Canada revealed a number of perceived barriers.[3] Among the most frequently cited are the following:

Foreign Investment-Screening Process

Japanese officials point repeatedly to the Foreign Investment Review Agency (FIRA) as a major obstacle to expanded investment in Canada. According to the high-level Survey Mission on the Overseas Investment Climate of Canada sent by Japan's Ministry of International Trade and Industry (MITI) in March-April 1982:

Table 6-1: *Canada-Japan Energy and Petrochemical Projects[a]*

		Japanese Firm(s)	Canadian Partner(s)	Amount	Status
LNG[b] Projects	1.	Nissho Iwai/Chubu Electric/Chugoku Electric/Kyushu Electric/Osaka Gas/Toho Gas	Dome Petroleum	2.9 MMT[c]	Basic agreement reached
	2.	Mitsui	PetroCanada/Westcoast	1-3 MMT	Feasibility study under way
	3.	C. Itoh	Alberta Consortium	3 MMT	Basic agreement reached
	4.	Sumitomo/Marubeni	Carter Energy	N/A[d]	Discussion stage
Crude oil, oil sands & heavy oil projects	5.	Arctic Petroleum, (60% JNOC)	Dome Petroleum	Loan	Agreement Signed
	6.	Japan Oil Sands (JOSCO) (52.4% JNOC)	Norcen		JOSCO has so far invested appr. $10 million for pilot-plant development work on *in situ* heavy oil recovery (Primrose).
	7.	Canada Oil Sands (CANOS) (80% JNOC)	PetroCanada/Cities Service/Esso Resources		CANOS has so far invested $30.8 million for pilot-plant development work on *in situ* oil-sand recovery.
Petro-chemical projects	8.	C. Itoh	Nova	N/A	Discussion stage
	9.	Mitsubishi	Dome/Occidental/Hooker	$2 billion	Feasibility study under way

Table 6-1 continued

	Japanese Firm(s)	Canadian Partner(s)	Amount	Status
10.	Idemitsu Petrochemical/ Nippon Petrochemical/ Toagosei Chemical/ Marubeni	N/A	N/A	Discussions
11.	Mitsubishi Petrochemical	Esso Chemical/Alberta Energy	N/A	Discussion stage
12.	Mitsui	Ocelot Industries	150,000 TPY*Methanol	Contracted from 1983
13.	Mitsui/Sumitomo	Alberta Gas Chemicals Canterra Energy Ltd.	N/A	Expansion of Alberta Methanol plant
LPG Project				
14.	Nikko LPG	Gulf Canada	240 000 Tons	Being imported under 5-year supply contract since 1966. Fourth 5-year contract is presently under negotiation
Thermal coal project				
15.	Ube Kosan/Mitsui	Luscar Ltd.-Coal Valley (Alta.)	300,000 TPY	5-year contract concluded (1980-84)
16.	Onoda Cement/Mitsui	Luscar Ltd.-Coal Valley (Alta.)	100,000 TPY	5-year contract concluded (1980-84)
17.	Toyo Soda/Mitsui	Luscar Ltd.-Coal Valley (Alta.)	50,000 TPY	5-year contract concluded (1980-84)
18.	Sumitomo Cement/ Sumitomo	Byron Creek-Coal Mountain (BC)	200,000 TPY	Delivery started 1980
19.	Nihon Cement/Marubeni	Coleman Collieries-Vicary Creek (BC)	100,000 TPY	Delivery started 1980
20.	Mitsui Mining/Tokyo Boeki	Denison Mines-Quintette (BC)	1 mill. TPY	Feasibility study; depends on outcome of current NEBC coking coal negotiations
21.	Sumitomo Coal Mining	Esso Resources (Alta.)	N/A	Feasibility study

Table 6-1 continued

	Japanese Firm(s)	Canadian Partner(s)	Amount	Status
22.	Electric Power Development Co.	Manalta Coal-McLeod River (Alta.)	2 mill. TPY	Feasibility study
23.	Chubu Electric Power Co.	Union Oil-Obed-Marsh (Alta.)	N/A	Feasibility study
24.	Idemitsu Kosan	Fording Coal-Shaughnessey (Alta.)	1 mill. TPY	Joint venture agreement signed
25.	Idemitsu Kosan	Manalta Coal-Mercoal (Alta.)	1 mill. TPY	Feasibility study
Uranium projects[h]				
26.	Taihei Uranium Exploration (Mitsubishi)		Y235 mill. invested	Exploration-Great Bear
27.	Uranium Development (Mitsui)		Y200 mill. invested	Exploration-Elliot Lake
28.	Ryowa Uranium Development (Mitsubishi)		Y100 mill. invested	Exploration-NWT
29.	Manitoba Uranium Development (Mitsui)		Y35 mill. invested	Exploration-Manitoba
30.	Saskatchewan Uranium Development (Mitsui)		Y84 mill. invested	Exploration-Sask.
31.	Northwest Uranium Development (Mitsui)		Y26 mill. invested	Exploration-NWT

Notes
a. Excluding coking coal.
b. LNG: Liquified natural gas.
c. MMT: Million tons.
d. N/A: Not applicable.
e. TPY: Tons per year.
f. LPG: Liquified petroleum gas.
g. NEBC: National Energy Board Canada.
h. Excluding existing supply contracts.

> The first problem encountered in making investment in Canada will be
> FIRA. In this connection, there are still problems in that the criteria for
> examination are not clearly defined, the duration of examination is too
> long, unreasonable undertakings are often called for, etc.[4]

Table 6-2 shows the disposition of Japanese applications to FIRA to
the end of July 1983; it indicates a disallowal rate marginally higher
for Japanese firms than for foreign applicants in general. Some
knowledgeable observers blame the higher Japanese rejection rate
more on communication problems than on substance. Japanese companies have been reluctant to take advantage of FIRA's pre-
application counselling services, which might in some cases have fa-
cilitated the application process and improved the likelihood of
approval.

National Energy Policy

Canada's new National Energy Policy (NEP), announced in 1980, is
viewed as highly discouraging to Japanese hopes for participation in
a variety of energy and resource megaprojects. The NEP rules on
domestic control have no direct impact on Japanese firms, as few of
these have controlling interests in energy-related development projects. But by restricting foreign ownership and generally creating a
climate which discourages new capital formation, the NEP threatens
the cancellation or postponement of major projects in which Japanese
participation through minority-equity financing, loans, infrastucture
assistance, and sales contracts might function prominently.[5] As a not-
able example, the Cold Lake, Alberta, tar-sands project, in which
Japanese firms had invested more than $10 million, was abandoned in
early 1982.[6] In other projects, such as Arctic Petroleum's oil exploration in the Beaufort Sea, the Japanese partners are obliged to wait
until Canada achieves self-sufficiency in petroleum before realizing
any return on their investment, which could ultimately total more
than $1 billion. To the extent that the NEP causes delays or cancella-
tions in energy projects, the Japanese may have to wait years or even
decades longer than anticipated to see the fruits of their participation.

Federal-Provincial Jurisdiction Conflicts

Disputes between the federal and provincial governments over control
of natural resources and foreign investments add complexity and con-
fusion to Canada's investment climate. As the *Report* of the MITI
Survey Mission on the Overseas Investment Climate of Canada aptly
put it, "there are remarkable differences in basic lines and various
detailed policies between the Federal government and the various Provinces, as well as between Provinces."[7]

Table 6-2: *Summary of Resolved FIRA Cases as of 31 July 1983*

	All Cases			Japan		
	No. of Cases	% of Total	% of Total	No. of Cases	% of Total	% of Total
Acquisitions						
Allowed	2 259	92	84	25	89	80
Disallowed	205	8	8	3	11	10
Subtotal	2 464	100		28	100	10
Withdrawn	228		8	8		
Total	2 692		100	31		100
New Businesses						
Allowed	2 186	92	82	61	88	77
Disallowed	198	8	7	8	12	10
Subtotal	2 384	100		69	100	13
Withdrawn	297		11	10		
Total	2 681		100	79		100
Disallowed	403	8	7	11[a]	11	10
Subtotal	4 848	100	10	97	100	12
Withdrawn	525		100	13		100
Total	5 373			110		

Note:
a. Of seven disallowed cases resubmitted, five were allowed and two were disallowed a second time.

World-Market Conditions

Even under favourable world-market conditions, the discouraging investment climate fostered by the National Energy Policy would probably inhibit the scope of new Japanese participation in Canadian development projects, at least in the energy sectors. The potential damage is exacerbated by the global recession, accompanied by falling demand and prices for industrial raw materials in general.[8] As expectations of continued price increases in petroleum and other materials are scaled downward, the urgency with which Japan is pursuing new development projects abroad is also waning. This can mean more than merely marking time for a year or two until world economic conditions improve: once large mega-projects, such as Cold Lake, are scuttled, it may well be decades, if ever, before they are revived. Either the depressed world-market condition alone or the NEP impact alone would have moderated the enthusiasm of prospective Japanese investors. The two forces in combination may be devastating.

Domestic Market Conditions

As discussed earlier, the small size and high labour costs of the Canadian economy limit the prospects of major new investments in manufacturing either for the domestic market or for export.

Labour Unrest

The high incidence of work stoppage and labour unrest in Canada is often cited by Japanese as inhibiting the prospects for Canadian investment. The number of working days lost through strikes each year, on a per capita basis, is thirty times higher in Canada than in Japan.[9] Japanese managers interviewed in the present study fear strikes and militant unionism as a major operating problem and as a threat to the stable supply of materials. Related to these concerns are pervasive Japanese perceptions of low productivity and shoddy workmanship on the part of Canadian workers. These perceptions may, however, be changing. The recent MITI Task Force concluded that "Canadian labour presents no particular problems in terms of its availability and quality. Labour relations are apparently not bad on the whole, excepting strikes, etc. in the public sector."[10]

Infrastructure Problems

Inadequately developed transportation and port facilities hinder potential Japanese participation in some resource projects, particularly in the mining of coal and non-ferrous metals. Realization of British Columbia's North East Coal Development, for example, was made possible only after the federal and provincial governments agreed to hundreds of millions of dollars of expenditures on the development of rail lines and port facilities, and on other necessary improvements. Similar infrastructure inadequacies complicate proposed Japanese-Canadian projects relating to the development of petrochemicals and liquified natural gas. Even where existing transport facilities can be used, they are often hopelessly overcrowded. Movements of Western Canadian resources destined for Japan are often delayed by inadequate rail facilities, which are largely a consequence of the antiquated Crow's Nest Pass freight rate that has artificially suppressed railway revenues since the 1920s.

Other Bureaucratic Controls

Even after a potential Japanese investment receives the approval of FIRA, it may be effectively blocked by the licensing requirements of the federal or provincial Ministries responsible for the industrial sectors involved. In some industries, foreign participation is permitted in some phases, but precluded from others. As an example, foreigners may invest in fish *processing*, but are denied permits by the Department of Fisheries and Environment to particpate in fish *harvesting*, despite the view of Japanese investors that these phases are necessarily interrelated and should be treated together. Potential Japanese investors cite myriad other bureaucratic controls and regulations which have the effect of inhibiting investment in Canada. As an example, the Canadian Department of Manpower and Immigration has, until recently, limited work permits for Japanese managers to one year, too short a period for effective corporate planning and management. (These rules have subsequently been eased.) Japanese in Quebec report difficulties in obtaining permits for their children to attend English schools. For Japanese investors considering alternative plant locations in Canada or elsewhere, such factors, although minor in themselves, may help tip the balance toward other countries where bureaucratic controls are less stringent. Additional obstacles to Japanese participation in Canadian megaprojects include 'Buy Canadian' procurement policies of both the federal and provincial governments.[11]

Policy Implications for Canada

Canada remains a highly attractive trade and investment partner for Japan. The recent MITI Survey Mission on the Overseas Investment

Environment in Canada concluded that "Canada is one of the promising countries in the world for making foreign capital investment."[12]
Mr. S. Moriyama, leader of the Mission, characterized the present trade
relationship between the two countries as a "mutually complementary
one."[13]

The benefits to Canada of Japanese business involvement are doc-
umented extensively in this report. But problems still remain. Increasingly, Canadians are asking whether the gains from the 'mutually
complementary' relationship are equitably distributed, or whether the
benefits may be accruing much more to the Japanese side.

Japan clearly reaps major benefits from secure supplies of Canadian
raw materials and from access to the Canadian market for Japanese
manufactures. But Canadians probably gain far less. While the overall
trade balance between the two countries remains in Canada's favour,
the traditional pattern of exporting raw materials and importing
manufactured products relegates Canada to the status of a less-
developed country in relation to Japan. And Japanese investment,
although it is both large in amount and significant to Canada, flows
almost exclusively into generating additional exports of raw materials, frustrating Canada's desire to achieve greater economic diversifi-
cation and domestic value added.

Canadians are justified in harbouring ambiguous feelings towards
Japanese business. At best, the relationship is a mixed blessing. From
Canada's perspective, substantial shortcomings remain, both in the
short term and in the long term. These inadequacies pose some hard
dilemmas for Canadian policy makers.

Trade Policies

The short-term problems are chiefly trade-related, focusing on three
main issues:
• Disruptive imports from Japan
• Inadequate local sourcing
• Impediments to Canadian manufactured exports.

Canadian concerns over Japanese imports are dominated by those
related to autos. The Japanese sell more than $1.5 billion-worth of
cars and parts annually in Canada, while they buy only $7 million
worth of Canadian automotive products. Even in the best of times,
such a gross imbalance would concern Canadians. But in the current
situation of severe recession in the domestic industry, the spectacular
surge of automotive imports from Japan is a highly visible irritant to
Canadians. Japanese business and government leaders speak repeatedly of their desire for mutually constructive economic relations with

Canada. Yet their apparent insensitivity to the plight of Canada's economy in general, and that of its auto industry in particular, disturbs and baffles Canadians. Japanese managers are admired for their ability to place long-term planning considerations above short-term profits. In the present crisis, however, they appear unwittingly to be doing the opposite: that is, creating ill will, resentment and possibly future controls by Canada, to gain a short-term advantage which many Canadians see as opportunistic and unfair.

The Canadian government's response to the flood of Japanese auto imports has been restrained so far by two factors: Canada's traditional adherence to free trade and its lack of a national consensus on appropriate control measures. Pressure for import controls is strongest in the auto-producing provinces of Ontario and Quebec, and considerably weaker elsewhere, where consumers want freedom of choice to buy the best cars available at the lowest possible price. A shaky compromise quota was agreed upon for 1982 only after Canadian Customs began delaying the entry of Japanese autos into Canada. A subsequent agreement extended import controls to the end of March 1984. Japanese officials have repeatedly asserted that they will not agree to any further extension of auto-import limits beyond that date, and Canada's case for further controls is likely to weaken with renewed growth of the Canadian economy. Nevertheless, unless the Japanese cooperate to ensure an orderly flow of auto exports, the Government of Canada will be under increasing public pressure to impose unilateral import controls in this area.

Japanese reluctance to obtain parts and supplies from Canada also focuses mainly on autos. Canada is the world's sixth-largest market for autos. Japanese producers manufacture in a number of smaller countries which have imposed import limits, and they presumably could do so in Canada, too. Short of actually manufacturing autos in Canada, Japanese producers could at least obtain more auto parts from Canadian suppliers without major cost effects; but even that is not being done.

Canada is understandably reluctant to impose local-content requirements, which fly in the face of free trade. But given the massive volume of automotive imports and the apparent insensitivity of the Japanese to deep-seated Canadian wishes, Canada may have more to gain than to lose by imposing modest Canadian-content requirements in the automotive sector. One encouraging sign was the recent announcement that Toyota will construct a small plant near Vancouver, BC, to manufacture aluminum wheels. The plant, involving a total planned investment of $23 million, is designed to produce 20 000 wheels per month and to employ some 100 persons.[14]

The problem of expanding Canadian-manufactured exports to Japan is a longer-term question which will require effort and good will from both sides. The Canadian government and some provinces have initiated major trade-promotion programs in Japan. Impediments to success exist on both sides. Despite sincere efforts by Japan to liberalize trade, it is a common perception that the Japanese still impose substantial non-tariff barriers, such as customs requirements, product standards, and 'buy-local' sentiments, against Canadian imports. At the same time, Canadians must share the blame for the present situation. Very few Canadian producers have been willing to invest the time and energy needed to develop an effective presence in the complex Japanese market. Their most common error is to assume that a product will 'sell itself' if the price is right, whereas competition in Japan is often based much more on quality and service than on price. Continued efforts by the Japanese to streamline import procedures, combined with Canadian efforts to facilitate communication between Canadian producers and prospective Japanese customers, lend optimism to expectations of some increase in Canadian-manufactured exports, particularly of electronic goods. But prospects for any significant upgrading of manufactured exports in the near future seem slight. As one of the very few countries of the world realizing a *surplus* in the overall value of its trade with Japan, Canada is not in a strong position to push the Japanese into buying more.

Indeed, there are some indications that Canadians should be concerned about maintaining even their traditional resource-based exports to Japan. N. Gregor Guthrie, President of the Canada-Japan Trade Council, points out that new Japanese developments in the application of micro-electronics pose a clear threat to Canada's copper exports.[15] As an example, Toyota is replacing copper wiring in its cars with fibre optics. Another long-term victim of Japanese technological advances may be Canadian exports of coking coal. The world's largest steel producer, Japan already has in place a twenty-year plan to substitute other materials for steel in its manufactured products. The development and successful testing of a ceramic automobile engine and intensive efforts to adapt synthetic fibre materials to replace steel in automobile bodies undoubtedly are contributing to this change.[16]

Investment Policies

On the investment side, Japanese participation is highly important to a number of Canada's major plans for megaprojects. The willingness of Japanese firms to share in the costs and risks of the development of new resources, without seeking operational control, fits harmoniously with Canadian objectives. But even here, some difficult policy options are posed for Canada.

In the first place, Canadians need to appraise clearly the nature of the benefits accruing from Japanese investments. Japanese officials speak a great deal about their ability to supply valuable technology and management skills to Canada. But the record to date is rather different. The Japanese have provided capital and purchase contracts, which are, as discussed earlier in this report, of great importance, but their contributions of technology and management techniques have been minimal. This may, of course, change, with the promise of Japanese participation in more technically advanced projects such as the development of petrochemicals and liquified natural gas (LNG). But based on the Japanese performance to date, Canadian policy makers should probably limit their expectations of Japanese contributions to megaprojects to infusion of capital and the conclusion of purchase contracts.

Although the Japanese have contributed significantly to resource-development projects in Canada, they have done virtually nothing to promote, or to assist in, the development of materials *processing* in Canada. Major plans are under discussion for the development of petrochemicals and other resource-related manufacturing projects. But many Canadians believe that their governments have not done enough to exert pressure on the Japanese to process materials in Canada. Raw materials are clearly one of Canada's greatest assets. To allow them to be exported in raw or unprocessed form is to forgo a vast potential for generating employment, developing skills, and creating higher domestic value added. Canada's bargaining power is, unquestionably, limited. Most of the materials which Canada exports to Japan face growing competition from other countries, particularly Australia and China. To the extent that the Japanese succeed in diversifying their sources, Canada's ability to bargain by implicit threats of withholding supplies becomes weaker. On the other hand, Canada has vast supplies to offer and, even more important, it offers political stability, a well-developed economic and physical infrastructure, and a highly skilled labour force. The Canadian federal and provincial governments, acting in unison, could probably exert more effective bargaining power than they have exerted in the past, to pressure Japanese companies into a greater range of 'downstream' processing in return for access to Canadian raw materials.

A related area of concern is the dearth of Japanese involvement in Canadian manufacturing sectors, other than in projects directly related to resource development. Although the lack of manufacturing

investment concerns Canadians, there is probably little that governments can do to alter the situation, based as it is on underlying economic realities of a small market size and high labour costs. Surprisingly, many Japanese businessmen seem unaware that under the 1979
GATT agreement, by January 1987, 80 per cent of Canadian exports
to the United States will enter duty free, and up to 95 per cent will be
subject to tariffs of 5 per cent or less.[17] Canada's federal and provincial
governments could probably promote more aggressively the advan-
tages for Japanese companies in using Canada as a manufacturing
base for the United States (US) market.

As discussed earlier, the Japanese frequently cite FIRA as a deterrent
to expanded investment. But Canada's foreign-investment screening
mechanism is no more restrictive or burdensome than those of many
other countries, and its function of insuring Canadian benefit is
needed. If the Japanese problems with FIRA result partially from
inadequate pre-application consultation, as seems likely, FIRA could
take a major step towards facilitating the investment the Japanese
wish to make by establishing an advisory office in Tokyo, or at least by
making periodic informational visits to Japan.

The Elusive Alliance: A Personal Conclusion

During more than eighteen months of work on the present report, the
author has held disucssions with literally hundreds of individuals,
both Japanese and Canadian. Two conclusions stand out vividly. The
first is that seldom in modern history have the needs and capacities of
two countries complemented each other as fully as in present-day
Canada and Japan. The potential for further Japanese business
involvement in Canada, to the mutual advantage of *both* sides, is
enormous. The second conclusion is that if the full potential of this
opportunity is to be realized, a change of attitude, or at least fuller
awareness of the existing possibilities, is called for from both sides.

It is important, first, that Canadians learn to differentiate among
the various origins and motives of foreign business involvement. It
seems obvious, for example, that the consequences of Japanese business in Canada are essentially benign: such business assists in the
development and stable marketing of Canada's resources, and supplies
Canadians with high-quality, reasonably priced products. Basically,
both of these benefits are in the interests of most Canadians. The goal
of Japanese business is distinctly *not* to secure management control
over major segments of the Canadian economy, as has come about
from US investment. The same types of 'knee-jerk' nationalistic de-

fenses and barriers that Canadians have erected against American business may be inappropriate and even self-defeating when applied to the Japanese.

The second imperative is that Japanese managers and public officials become more sensitive to the needs and perceptions of Canadians. Rightly or wrongly, there is a widespread belief among Canadians that Japanese decision makers are impervious to Canadian demands for more value added to resources before they are exported, for more sourcing of parts in Canada, and for moderation in the import of Japanese manufactures which compete with and displace Canadian-made products at home.

Canadians are deeply concerned about these issues, which strike not only at their economic well-being, but also at their sense of national pride and dignity. It is of little consequence that there may also be exploitive elements in Canada's economic relations with other countries. Unlike Americans and Europeans, the Japanese are a new and unknown presence in Canada. The burden of proof lies with them to convince a suspicious Canadian public that their involvement is consistent with Canada's needs. The Japanese can easily afford to upgrade Canadian value added in their imports and to maintain a more orderly flow of manufactured exports to Canada. Their failure to do so can only fuel resentment and generate pressure for controls and restrictions.

Without these changes in attitudes and perceptions, the full symbiotic benefit of the Canadian-Japanese business alliance is likely to remain unrealized. But the potential for a mutually rewarding, nonthreatening relationship is there. Whether there will be enough sensitivity and flexibility on both sides remains to be seen. As interaction and awareness grow between Canada and Japan, we may hope that this elusive alliance will mature to reach its full potential.

Notes

1. "B.C. Picks Dome Pete for LNG Project," *Globe and Mail* (Toronto), 16 July 1982, p. B1.

2. "Two more bids for gas projects filed in B.C.," *Star* (Toronto), 2 December 1981, p. D18.

3. See also R. W. Wright, "Foreign Investment Between Neighbours: Canada and Japan."

4. Japan, Ministry of International Trade and Industry (MITI), Survey Mission on Overseas Investment Environment to Canada, *Report of the Survey Mission on Overseas Investment Environment to Canada*, p. 8.

5. "Megaproject failures mean high policy changes," *Financial Post*, 8 May 1982, p. 1.

6.   "Obstacles keep sands projects from becoming reality," *Globe and Mail*, 8 March 1982, p. R14.

7.   MITI, *Report of the Survey Mission*, p. 8.

8.   "Oil price slump slows energy project plans," *Financial Post*, 31 January 1982, p. 1.

9.   MITI, *Report of the Survey Mission*, p. 107.

10.   MITI, *Report of the Survey Mission*, p. 10.

11.   "Companies pushed to shop at home," *Financial Post*, 15 May 1982, p. 4. Gulf Canada Resources announced in April 1982 that it had decided to accept a Japanese bid for $32 million in prefabricated buildings for drilling islands in the Beaufort Sea. The federal Office of Industrial and Regional Benefits (OIRB) asked Gulf to reopen bids, for a longer period, to give Canadian companies more opportunity to bid. Eventually, Gulf awarded the contract to Dominion Bridge Co.

12.   MITI, *Report of the Survey Mission*, p. 44.

13.   "Canada-Japan trade needs: Are they compatible?," *Star*, 6 April 1982), p. C2.

14.   "Go-ahead seen for Toyota plant," *Globe and Mail*, 10 November 1982, p. B5.

15.   N. G. Guthrie, "Canada's Trade with Japan in a Future Fraught with Change."

16.   Guthrie, "Canada's Trade."

17.   Canada, Standing Senate Committee on Foreign Affairs, *Canada-United States Relations, Volume 3: Canada's Trade Relations with the United States*, p. 9.

Appendix A: A Note on the Use of Input-Output Models

This note is designed to give the average reader a concise introduction to the technique of input-output analysis, with specific focus on the Statistics Canada input-output models used in this research. It assumes no knowledge of econometrics on the part of the reader and thus for some, may be too elementary. The goal is, however, that any interested reader be able to understand the methodology used, and the discussion is therefore directed toward the least-informed reader.

An input-output matrix is an explicit picture of transactions among industries and consumers in an economy. An example would be provided by considering the place of lumber in Canada's economy. Lumber is used by a variety of industries, as well as by households. It is conceivably possible to measure the total consumption of lumber by adding up the consumption of lumber by each industry and its consumption by individuals. Included would be the amount of lumber used in the manufacture of pulp and paper, newprint, cellulose, construction, heating, shipbuilding, and so on. By extension, a larger table could be drawn up, showing in detail the consumption of all products in all industries of the economy. Burdensome as it may sound, this is precisely the task performed by the Structural Analysis Division of Statistics Canada, which generates this information across 191 industries, 595 commodities, 136 categories of final consumers, and seven primary inputs (such as labour).

Once these tables have been developed, it is easy to see, for example, how many newspapers were printed, consuming what quantities of logs, chemicals, ink and other materials. Even less evident inputs and their quantities, such as steel for the machinery and wire for the circuits, can be isolated, as can key inputs such as labour and electricity. The sum of all these inputs can be attributed directly to the production of newspapers.

89

Once these relationships are known, it is a simple mathematical calculation to identify direct and indirect demand generated by the production of one more, or one less, newspaper. Or, on a larger scale, it is possible to examine the net generation of demand by all the newspapers printed by all the publishers in Canada.

Taking the analysis one step further, it is possible to aggregate the economic impact of any business or group of businesses. In the present research, the focus has been on the direct and indirect impact of the group of Canadian-domiciled businesses with direct Japanese participation.

For this study, the computerized National and Provincial Input-Output Models available in Ottawa were used, with the assistance of Statistics Canada personnel. The inputs used in running the National model were the number of employees and/or sales volume for each firm, and the nature of its main activity (by Standard Industrial Classification code). The program was able to isolate the direct and indirect impact of each group of Japanese companies on 191 industries in Canada. As the degree of detail obtainable is too fine for the purposes of this document, the results obtained were aggregated down to sixteen industries, forty-nine commodities, and fourteen categories of final demand. The commodity breakdown is not presented in the text, as it is not germane to the main thrust of the discussion.

A similar simulation exercise was performed on the Statistics Canada Provincial model, using the same informational inputs plus a geographic identification of each company's activity. The results show the distribution of the direct and indirect impact of Japanese business activity in each of the provinces of Canada.

It is important to note that this analysis makes the inherent assumption that Japanese businesses in Canada do not behave substantially differently, in terms of input-consumption patterns, from Canadian businesses in Canada of comparable activity and size. For most categories, this assumption appears reasonable, and standard Canadian profiles were used in the analysis. However, preliminary studies suggested that this assumption is less valid in the Trading and Merchandising sectors, where Japanese companies in Canada appear to operate with substantially lower margins than do Canadian traders and wholesales. In the Statistics Canada models, gross sales volumes are generally used as the input to compute sales margins (or value added), according to average domestic industry standards. The sales margins, in turn, serve as the base for projecting the consumption of goods and services (or economic impact). If the Japanese trading firms in Canada operate on a lower sales margin than their domestically-owned counterparts, use of their gross sales figures in the models would yield an exaggerated statement of their impact. Consequently, the average margin figures from the standard Canadian tables were replaced in this study with estimates extrapolated directly from the published balance sheets of the larger Japanese trading houses and merchandising companies in Canada. These results are presented in the text.

Readers interested in a more detailed description of input-output analysis are directed to *Input-Output Analysis: A Non-Technical Description* (the Conference Board in Canada, 1971). Statistics Canada also publishes annually a more technical explanation of their models in *The Input-Output Structure of the Canadian Economy* (Statistics Canada catalog number 15-201E).

Appendix B: Japanese Ownership of Canadian Companies

One of the most frustrating problems in studying Japanese business in Canada is the difficulty of obtaining a comprehensive and reliable directory of Japanese-owned companies in Canada. The company listings in Chapter 3 of this report were drawn from a wide range of published sources and personal contacts.

Among the most useful indexes of foreign ownership in Canada is *Inter-Corporate Ownership (ICO)*, published by Statistics Canada. The information it contains is based primarily on non-confidential returns filed by Canadian corporations under the Corporations and Labour Unions Returns Act (CALURA), supplemented by other published sources. It is a comprehesive index of who owns and/or controls what business(es) in Canada. It summarizes both direct and ultimate non-resident ownership for each foreign country and includes individual as well as corporate shareholders.

The Non-Resident Ownership section of the 1982 *ICO* lists 141 Canadian companies controlled directly or ultimately from Japan, and another 85 with non-controlling Japanese-ownership participation. Although the ownership information contained in the 1982 directory is principally a final 1979 version, all major take-overs and changes known to have occurred during 1980 have been included.

The lists below have been reproduced from *ICO 1982*. This is not necessarily a complete or up-to-date inventory. Many of the companies on the list are unknown to the author, despite extensive investigation, and other companies listed are known to have terminated operations. The author considers, nevertheless, that the list will be a useful complement to the information presented elsewhere in this report.

93

The first portion of the list below is an alphabetical index of Japanese-controlled companies in Canada; the second portion lists non-controlled companies with Japanese ownership. Column 1 indicates the proportion of *direct* Japanese ownership. Column 2 indicates the extent of *ultimate* ownership. Column 3 indicates province of residence, and column 4 reveals the nature of activity, by Standard Industrial Classification (SIC).

Japanese Controlled Companies in Canada

D%	U%	RES	SIC	Corporation Name
100.0	100.0	BC	111	Aero International Enterprises Ltd.
50.0	50.0	Que.	625	Alpac Aluminum Limited/ALPAC
100.0	100.0	Ont.	619	Alspeed Products Limited
0.0	40.0	BC	517	Annacis Auto Terminals Ltd.
0.0	100.0	Ont.	656	Bahr Auto Sales Limited
0.0	100.0	Ont.	656	Brennan Brothers Motors Limited
100.0	100.0	BC	619	Bridgestone Tire Co. Canada Ltd.
50.0	100.0	Que.	623	Brother International Corp. Canada Ltd.
100.0	100.0	Ont.	617	C. Itoh & Co.(Canada) Ltd.
100.0	100.0	Ont.	623	C. Itoh Industrial Machinery Canada Ltd.
100.0	100.0	Ont.	623	C. Itho Mining Company Canada Ltd.
100.0	100.0	Ont.	404	Canadian Hitachi Plant Construction Co.
0.0	100.0	Ont.	619	Canadian Kawasaki Motors Limited
100.0	100.0	Ont.	625	Canadian Koyo Co. Ltd.
0.0	89.9	Ont.	623	Canon Optics and Business Machines Canada Ltd.
0.0	99.8	BC	623	Carette Automobiles (1979) Ltée
100.0	100.0	Que.	617	Chori Canada Limited
100.0	100.0	Que.	617	Chori Ontario Limited
0.0	67.0	Que.	617	Compagnie de Chaussures Consolidée Ltée
100.0	100.0	BC	251	CIPA Lumber Co. Ltd.
50.0	50.0	Que.	239	Cirtex Knitting Inc.
54.1	54.1	BC	251	Crestbrook Forest Industries Ltd.
0.0	54.1	BC	756	Crestbrook Pulp and Paper Ltd.
100.0	100.0	BC	756	CTC Trading Ltd.
100.0	100.0	BC	271	Daishowa-Marubeni International Limited
0.0	100.0	Que.	656	Datsun Fairview Limited
100.0	100.0	BC	656	Diahakone Kankoo-Jigyo Co. Ltd.
100.0	100.0	Ont.	099	Domik Exploration Limited
100.0	100.0	Ont.	656	Don Valley North Toyota Limited
100.0	100.0	BC	094	Dowa Mining Co. Ltd.
0.0	100.0	Ont.	656	Eglinton East Toyota Ltd.
100.0	100.0	Ont.	629	Elmo Canada Mfg. Corp.
100.0	100.0	BC	756	Emachy Lumber Co. Ltd.
100.0	100.0	Ont.	335	Erie Technological Products Limited
0.0	100.0	Que.	656	Fairview Toyota Inc.
0.0	100.0	Ont.	756	Featherlite Leisure Products Incorporated
0.0	54.1	BC	756	Fort Plywood & Lumber Ltd.
100.0	100.0	BC	505	Fraser Wharves Ltd.
66.7	66.7	Que.	505	Fuji Photo Film Canada Inc.
100.0	100.0	BC	505	Fuji Trading Company Ltd.
76.5	76.5	Que.	218	Fujitex Ltd.
0.0	100.0	BC	218	Fung Lin Enterprises Ltd.

D%	U%	RES	SIC	Corporation Name
100.0	100.0	Ont.	699	HIC Canada Ltd.
95.0	100.0	BC	324	Himac Motors Ltd.
100.0	100.0	Ont.	324	Hitachi (Canadian) Ltd.
100.0	100.0	Ont.	623	Hitachi Construction Machinery Canada Ltd.
99.6	99.6	Ont.	676	Hitachi Denshi Ltd.
100.0	100.0	Que.	621	Hitachi (HSC) Canada Inc.
100.0	100.0	Ont.	619	Honda Canada Inc.
0.0	100.0	BC	619	International Diahakone Investments Ltd.
100.0	100.0	Que.	619	Itoman (Canada) Inc.
0.0	100.0	BC	619	J.C. Wright Limited
100.0	100.0	Alt.	619	Japan Canada Oil Sands Limited
100.0	100.0	Alt.	064	Japan Oil Sands Company Primrose Limited
100.0	100.0	BC	756	Japan-Alberta Oil Mill Co. Ltd.
100.0	100.0	Alt.	756	Japex Canada Ltd.
100.0	100.0	Ont.	621	JVC Canada Inc.
100.0	100.0	BC	629	Kawasho International Canada Limited
0.0	100.0	Ont.	699	Ken Parisien Pianos Limited
0.0	100.0	Ont.	379	Kohl & Madden Printing Ink Company of Canada Limited
76.2	100.0	Ont.	623	Komatsu Canada Limited
80.0	100.0	Ont.	622	Kubota Tractor Canada Ltd.
0.0	100.0	Que.	622	Lasalle Mazda Ltd/Ltée
100.0	100.0	Alt.	623	M B L Sales Ltd.
100.0	100.0	Ont.	623	Makita Power Tools Canada Ltd.
100.0	100.0	BC	793	Marc Narod Enterprises Ltd.
100.0	100.0	Ont.	629	Marubeni Canada Limited
0.0	100.0	Ont.	621	Matsushita Electric of Canada Limited
100.0	100.0	Ont.	334	Matsushita Industrial Canada Ltd.
100.0	100.0	Ont.	619	Mazda Canada Inc.
50.0	50.0	BC	111	Millbanke Industries Limited
0.0	40.0	BC	111	Mini Truck Conversions Ltd.
0.0	100.0	Ont.	623	Minolta Business Equipment (Canada) Ltd.
50.0	50.0	Man.	254	Misawa Homes of Canada Ltd.
100.0	100.0	BC	625	Mitsubishi Canada Ltd.
100.0	100.0	Ont.	625	Mitsui and Company Canada Ltd.
100.0	100.0	BC	625	Mitsui Mining Canada Limited
0.0	100.0	Man.	699	MKB Music Ltd.
100.0	100.0	BC	623	Mycom Canada Ltd.
100.0	100.0	Ont.	623	N T N Bearing Corporation of Canada Ltd.
0.0	100.0	NS	656	NAC (Halifax) Limited
100.0	100.0	BC	031	Naden Harbour Timber Ltd.
99.0	99.0	Ont.	621	NGK Insulators of Canada Ltd.
99.7	99.7	Ont.	621	NGK Insulators of Canada Ltd.
99.9	99.9	Que.	629	Nichimen Canada Ltd.
100.0	100.0	BC	629	Nichimo Trading Company Ltd.
100.0	100.0	Ont.	619	Nippondenso Canada Ltd.
100.0	100.0	BC	619	Nissan Automobile Co. Canada Ltd.
0.0	100.0	BC	619	Nissan Leasing Ltd.
100.0	100.0	Ont.	617	Nissho-Iwai Canada Ltd.
90.0	90.0	Ont.	618	Noritake Canada Limited
0.0	98.5	BC	618	North Shore Datsun Ltd.
100.0	100.0	BC	618	Norzaki Trading Inc.
100.0	100.0	Ont.	623	NSK Bearing Canada Limited
87.1	100.0	Ont.	315	NTN Bearing Mfg. Canada Ltd.
100.0	100.0	BC	625	Okura & Co. Canada Ltd.

D%	U%	RES	SIC	Corporation Name
100.0	100.0	BC	625	P N C Exploration (Canada) Ltd.
36.2	70.2	BC	094	Pacific Coal Ltd.
100.0	100.0	BC	094	Pentax of Canada Ltd.
0.0	100.0	Ont.	094	Polychrome Corporation Canada Ltd.
100.0	100.0	Ont.	875	Prince Hotel Toronto Limited
0.0	100.0	Ont.	875	Pulsar Time Canada Inc.
50.8	50.8	BC	094	Quintette Coal Limited
100.0	100.0	NS	094	Richocean Trading Company Limited
50.0	50.0	Que.	334	Sanyo Canada Inc.
100.0	100.0	BC	334	Sato Canada Trading Ltd.
100.0	100.0	BC	334	Sea Pride Enterprises Ltd.
100.0	100.0	Ont.	791	Seibu Canada Limited
0.0	100.0	Ont.	629	Seiko Time Canada Ltd.
100.0	100.0	Ont.	621	Sharp Electronics of Canada Limited
100.0	100.0	Que.	617	Shinko Canada Ltd.
0.0	99.8	BC	617	Sinclair Datsun Sales (1976) Ltd.
50.0	50.0	Ont.	629	Spectro Electric Industry Inc.
60.0	60.0	BC	875	Suehiro Food Co. Ltd. (Canada)
76.7	100.0	BC	094	Sumac Mines Ltd.
100.0	100.0	BC	629	Sumiglass Products Ltd.
100.0	100.0	BC	625	Sumitomo Canada Limited
100.0	100.0	BC	094	Sumitomo Metal Mining Canada Ltd.
100.0	100.0	Ont.	619	Suzuki Canada Inc.
100.0	100.0	Nfl.	699	Taito Seiko Company Limited
100.0	100.0	Nfl.	504	Taiyo Canada Limited
100.0	100.0	Ont.	623	Takara Company Canada Ltd.
0.0	61.4	BC	305	Titan Steel and Wire Co. Ltd.
100.0	100.0	Ont.	305	The Tokio Marine and Fire Insurance Co.
100.0	100.0	Ont.	623	Tokyo Electric Canada Ltd.
100.0	100.0	Ont.	621	Toshiba of Canada Limited
100.0	100.0	BC	621	Toshiba International Corp. (Cdn. Br.)
100.0	100.0	Ont.	621	Toshiba Machine Company, America
100.0	100.0	Ont.	621	Tovan Investments Ltd.
88.9	88.9	BC	793	Townline Development Corp.
50.0	100.0	Ont.	629	Toyomenka Canada Ltd.
100.0	100.0	Ont.	629	Toyota Canada Inc.
100.0	100.0	BC	629	Tsuda Canada Ltd.
100.0	100.0	Ont.	629	Yamaha Canada Music Ltd.
100.0	100.0	Ont.	619	Yamaha Motor Canada Ltd.-Yamaha Moteur
100.0	100.0	Que.	741	Yamaichi International Canada Ltd.
100.0	100.0	Ont.	629	Yashica Canada Inc.
100.0	100.0	Que.	399	YKK Canada Ltd.
100.0	100.0	BC	619	Yokohama Tire Corporation
100.0	100.0	BC	619	Yoshi of Vancouver Ltd.
100.0	100.0	BC	625	Yuasa Shoji Co. Ltd.

Japanese Businesses in Canada (Uncontrolled)

D%	U%	RES	SIC	Corporation Name
0.0	6.4	Ont.	756	96130 Canada Ltd.
0.0	3.8	Que.	094	Abitibi Asbestos Mining Company Ltd.
19.4	19.4	BC	064	Aero Trading Co. Ltd.
49.0	49.0	BC	266	Akai Audio Video Canada Inc.

D%	U%	RES	SIC	Corporation Name
0.0	49.0	Que.	629	Anglophoto Instruments Ltd.
33.2	33.2	BC	061	B.C. Coal Ltd.
0.0	33.2	BC	791	Balmer Coal Limited
0.0	30.0	Que.	261	Belbois Ltd.
0.0	3.0	Alt.	756	Bethalta Resources Limited
3.1	3.1	BC	053	Bethlehem Copper Corporation
6.4	6.4	Nfl.	756	Brinco Limited
0.0	6.4	Alt.	756	Brinco Oil and Gas Ltd.
0.0	6.4	Ont.	756	Brinco Quebec Limited
0.0	6.4	Nfl.	756	Brinex Limited
0.0	42.8	Ont.	393	Campbell Golf Ball Co. Ltd.
7.3	7.3	Alt.	135	Canbra Foods Ltd.
0.0	14.7	BC	635	Canweld Fabrications Ltd.
49.8	49.8	BC	111	Cassiar Packing Company Ltd.
0.0	6.3	BC	071	Cassiar Resources Ltd.
2.5	2.5	Que.	756	Chateau Montlabert Inc.
21.6	21.6	Ont.	869	Consolidated Computer Inc.
0.0	33.2	BC	756	Crows Nest Coal Mines Ltd.
10.0	10.0	Sas.	315	Ebadisco Manufacturing Canada Limited
29.9	49.8	BC	031	Elk Trading Co. Ltd.
0.0	5.1	BC	869	Fernie Coal Mines Ltd.
25.0	25.0	BC	251	Finlay Forest Industries Ltd.
49.0	49.0	BC	756	Fontana Investments Ltd.
48.9	48.9	BC	629	Fontile Corp. Ltd.
0.0	7.3	Alt.	756	Golden Bell Foods Limited
0.0	30.0	Que.	621	Henry Galler and Co. Ltd.
7.8	7.8	Ont.	875	Hidden Valley Inn Limited
49.0	49.0	Ont.	409	Janome Sewing Machine Co. (Canada) Ltd.
0.0	49.0	Ont.	875	Japanese Village Limited
0.0	6.4	Alt.	064	Jasper Oils Ltd.
30.0	53.2	BC	094	Kaiser Coal Canada Ltd.
0.0	7.2	Ont.	614	Kemptville Foods Limited
0.0	33.2	BC	094	Kootenay Coal Contractors Ltd.
0.0	6.4	BC	094	Kutcho Creek Asbestos Co. Ltd.
45.0	45.0	BC	614	Marifuji Trading Co. Ltd.
40.0	40.0	BC	875	Mayo Forest Products Ltd.
49.0	49.0	Ont.	409	Minolta Camera (Canada) Inc.
0.0	33.2	BC	404	Mountain View Realty Ltd.
49.0	49.0	Ont.	756	Nikon Canada Inc.
32.1	32.1	Ont.	756	Nipcan International Limited
0.0	28.5	BC	041	Norango Fishing Ltd.
0.0	28.5	BC	111	Norpac Fisheries Ltd.
12.0	12.0	BC	094	NRD Mining Ltd. NPL.
17.4	17.4	BC	094	Nuspar Resources Ltd.
0.0	49.9	BC	793	Oakland Fisheries Ltd.
0.0	49.0	BC	791	Oakland Industries Ltd.
0.0	25.0	BC	699	Pacific Net & Twine Ltd.
50.0	50.0	BC	869	Pisces Trading Company Limited
0.0	33.2	BC	756	Plateau Resources Ltd.
0.0	35.0	BC	111	Port Alberni Fish Co. (1976) Ltd.
30.0	30.0	Que.	629	Rezbond Abrasives Co. Ltd.
10.0	40.0	Que.	243	Rubin Bros. (Clothiers) Ltd.
0.0	7.3	Ont.	608	S.F. Foods Limited
49.0	49.0	BC	864	Sanei Investments Ltd.
13.5	13.5	BC	094	Saxon Coal Limited

D%	U%	RES	SIC	Corporation Name
25.0	25.0	Man.	393	Sekine Canada Limited
0.0	10.0	BC	094	Sheba Copper Mines Ltd.
49.0	49.0	Man.	621	Sony of Canada Ltd.
25.0	25.0	Que.	756	Southeast Asia Bauxites Ltd.
0.0	7.0	Ont.	139	Stafford Foods Ltd.
0.0	6.3	BC	899	Territorial Supply Company Limited
0.0	35.0	BC	111	Tofino Packing Co. 1965 Ltd.
0.0	48.0	BC	727	Tohcan Canada Limited
48.0	48.0	BC	727	Tohcan Limited
0.0	48.0	BC	727	Tohcan Services Limited
35.0	35.0	BC	727	Tohto Ocean Commerce Limited
20.0	35.0	BC	111	Tonquin Enterprises Ltd.
14.0	37.0	BC	517	Transpacific Tours Limited
0.0	14.7	BC	404	Tree Island Construction Limited
0.0	14.7	BC	305	Tree Island Steel Co. Ltd.
0.0	14.7	BC	629	Trisco Trading Ltd.
33.3	33.3	Alt.	139	United Oilseed Products Ltd.
39.0	39.0	BC	791	Versatile Cold Storage Corporation
9.0	9.8	BC	111	Wescan Fisheries Ltd.
0.0	14.3	BC	111	Western Pacific Sea Foods Ltd.
0.0	33.2	BC	505	Westshore Terminals Ltd.
25.0	25.0	Ont.	791	Zur Son Holdings Ltd.

Bibliography

Bruk, John. *Asia Pacific Foundation.* A study prepared for the Secretary of State for External Affairs. 23 September 1982.

Conservation of Human Resource Project, Columbia University, in co-operation with the Japan Society Inc. *Economic Impact of the Japanese Business Community in the United States.* New York: Japan Society Inc., 1979.

Financial Post, 30 January; 8, 15 May; 12 June 1982.

Financial Times (Canada), 14 September; 9 November 1981.

Gazette (Montreal), 3 October 1981.

Gherson, Joan. "Japanese Investment in Canada." *Foreign Investment Review* 3 (Autumn 1979): 4-7.

Globe and Mail (Toronto), December 1981-September 1983.

Guthrie, N. Gregor. "Canada's Trade with Japan in a Future Fraught with Change." Address at Port of Halifax Day 1982, Hotel Nova Scotian, Halifax, N.S., 13 September 1982.

Harbridge House Inc. *The Imported Automobile Industry in Canada: An assessment of key aspects of its impact on the Canadian Economy and the Canadian Consumer.* Boston: Harbridge House Inc., 1980.

Knight, Susan. *Japan's Expanding Manufacturing Presence in the United States: A Profile.* Washington: Japan Economic Institute of America, 1980.

Litvak, Isaiah A. et al. *Dual Loyalty: Canadian-US Business Arrangements.* Toronto: McGraw-Hill, 1971.

Oriental Economist (Toyo Keizai Shinposha). Japanese Overseas Investment: A Complete Listing by Firms and Countries, 1982. Tokyo: Toyo Keizai Shinposha Ltd., 1982. (This is an English translation of the annual publication *Kaigaishinshutsu Kigyo Soran.*)

Province (Vancouver), 30 June 1982.

Rugman, Alan M. *Multinationals in Canada: Theory, Performance, and Economic Impact.* Boston: Martinus Nijhoff Publishing, 1980.

Safarin, A.E. *The Performance of Foreign Owned Firms in Canada.* Washington: Canadian-American Committee, 1969.

Standing Senate Committee on Foreign Affairs (Canada). *Canada-United States Relations, Volume 3: Canada's Trade Relations with the United States.* Ottawa: Standing Senate Committee on Foreign Affairs, 1975-1982.

Star (Toronto), 2 December 1981; 6 April 1982.

Statistics Canada, Business Finance Division. *Inter-Corporate Ownership: 1980.* Ottawa: Statistics Canada, Business Finance Division, 1981.

Sun (Vancouver), 30 June; 3 July 1982.

Survey Mission on Overseas Investment Environment to Canada, Ministry of International Trade and Industry, Japan (MITI). *Report of the Survey Mission on Overseas Investment Environment to Canada, March 27-April 10, 1982.* Tokyo: Japan Overseas Enterprises Association, 1982. (translated from Japanese)

Tsurumi, Yoshi with Tsurumi, Rebecca R. *Sogoshosha: Engines of Export-Based Growth.* (2d ed.) Montreal: Institute for Research on Public Policy, 1984.

Wright, Richard W. "Canadian Joint Ventures in Japan." *Business Quarterly* 42 (Autumn 1977): 42-53.

Wright, Richard W. "Foreign Investment Between Neighbours: Canada and Japan" in *Canadian Perspectives on Economic Relations with Japan,* edited by Keith A.J. Hay, pp. 191-202. Montreal: Institute for Research on Public Policy, 1980.

Wright, Richard W. "Japan's Investment in Canada." *Business Quarterly* 41 (Summer 1976): 20-27.

The Members of the Institute

Board of Directors

The Honourable John B. Aird, O.C., Q.C.
  (Honorary Chairman)
  Lieutenant Governor of Ontario, Toronto
The Honourable Robert L. Stanfield, P.C.,
  Q.C. (Chairman), Ottawa
Louis A. Desrochers, Q.C. (Vice-Chairman)
  McCuaig, Desrochers, Edmonton
Richard Cashin
  President, Newfoundland Fishermen, Food
  and Allied Workers' Union, St. John's
Claude Castonguay, C.C.
  Président et chef de la direction,
  La Corporation du Groupe
  La Laurentienne, Québec
Guy Chabot, C.A.
  Raymond, Chabot, Martin & Paré
  Montréal
Roger Charbonneau
  Président du conseil d'administration
  Banque Nationale de Paris (Canada)
  Montréal
Dr. Rod Dobell
  President, The Institute for Research on
  Public Policy, Victoria
Dr. Henry E. Duckworth, O.C.
  President Emeritus
  University of Winnipeg
Dr. Regis Duffy
  President, Diagnostic Chemicals Ltd.
  Charlottetown
Dr. James D. Fleck
  Faculty of Management Studies
  University of Toronto
Peter C. Godsoe
  Vice Chairman, The Bank of Nova Scotia
  Toronto
The Honourable William M. Hamilton,
  P.C., O.C., LL.D., Royal Commission on
  the Economic Union and Development
  Prospects for Canada, Vancouver
Grace Hartman
  President Emeritus, CUPE, Willowdale
David Hennigar
  Atlantic Regional Director
  Burns Fry Limited, Halifax

T. E. Kierans
  President, McLeod Young Weir Limited
  Toronto
Roland J. Lutes, C.A.
  Clarkson, Gordon, Saint John
E.M. Mills
  Director, Calgary Chamber of Commerce
Pierre Nadeau
  Président du conseil, Tioxide Canada Inc.
  Montréal
Dr. Tom Pepper
  Pepper Consultants Ltd., Saskatoon
Guy Roberge, Q.C., Conseil
  Clarkson, Tétrault, Ottawa
Claudine Sotiau
  Ducros, Meilleur, Roy et associés ltée
  Montréal

Secretary
Peter C. Dobell
  Director, Parliamentary Centre
  for Foreign Affairs and Foreign Trade
  Ottawa

Treasurer
Dr. Louis Vagianos
  Executive Director, The Institute for
  Research on Public Policy, Halifax

Executive Committee
The Honourable Robert L. Stanfield
  (Chairman)
Louis A. Desrochers (Vice-Chairman)
Claude Castonguay
Peter C. Dobell
Rod Dobell
Roland J. Lutes
Louis Vagianos

Investment Committee
Tom Kierans (Chairman)
Marcel Cazavan
Peter C. Dobell
Peter C. Godsoe
Paul Little

Council of Trustees

Institute Management

Rod Dobell	President
Louis Vagianos	Executive Director
Gordon Robertson	Fellow-in-Residence
John M. Curtis	Director, International Economics Program
Gérald d'Amboise	Director, Small- and Medium-Sized Business Program
Barbara L. Hodgins	Director, Western Resources Program
Barry Lesser	Director, Regional Employment Opportunities Program
Louis Vagianos	Acting Director, Technology and Society Program
Parker Staples	Director, Financial Services
Donald Wilson	Director, Communications
Tom Kent	Editor, *Policy Options Politiques*

The Institute for Research on Public Policy
Publications Available
November 1984

Leroy O. Stone & Claude Marceau	*Canadian Population Trends and Public Policy Through the 1980s.* 1977 $4.00
Raymond Breton	*The Canadian Condition: A Guide to Research in Public Policy.* 1977 $2.95
Raymond Breton	*Une orientation de la recherche politique dans le contexte canadien.* 1977 $2.95
J.W. Rowley & W.T. Stanbury (eds.)	*Competition Policy in Canada: Stage II, Bill C-13.* 1978 $12.95
W.E. Cundiff	*Nodule Shock? Seabed Mining and the Future of the Canadian Nickel Industry.* 1978 $3.00
C.F. Smart & W.T. Stanbury (eds.)	*Studies on Crisis Management.* 1978 $9.95
W.T. Stanbury (ed.)	*Studies on Regulation in Canada.* 1978 $9.95
Michael Hudson	*Canada in the New Monetary Order: Borrow? Devalue? Restructure!* 1978 $6.95
Robert A. Russel	*The Electronic Briefcase: The Office of the Future.* 1978 $3.00
C.C. Gotlieb	*Computers in the Home: What They Can Do for Us—And to Us.* 1978 $3.00
David K. Foot (ed.)	*Public Employment and Compensation in Canada: Myths and Realities.* 1978 $10.95
Raymond Breton & Gail Grant Akian	*Urban Institutions and People of Indian Ancestry: Suggestions for Research.* 1979 $3.00
K.A. J. Hay	*Friends or Acquaintances? Canada and Japan's Other Trading Partners in the Early 1980s.* 1979 $3.00
Thomas H. Atkinson	*Trends in Life Satisfaction Among Canadians, 1968-1977.* 1979 $3.00
W.E. Cundiff & Mado Reid (eds.)	*Issues in Canadian/U.S. Transborder Computer Data Flows.* 1979 $6.50
David K. Foot (ed.)	*Public Employment in Canada: Statistical Series.* 1979 $15.00

Meyer W. Bucovetsky (ed.)	*Studies in Public Employment and Compensation in Canada.* 1979 $14.95
Richard French & André Béliveau	*The RCMP and the Management of National Security.* 1979 $6.95
Richard French & André Béliveau	*La GRC et la gestion de la sécurité nationale.* 1979 $6.95
Fred Thompson & W.T. Stanbury	*The Political Economy of Interest Groups in the Legislative Process in Canada.* 1979 $3.00
G. Bruce Doern & Allan M. Maslove (eds.)	*The Public Evaluation of Government Spending.* 1979 $10.95
Leroy O. Stone & Michael J. MacLean	*Future Income Prospects for Canada's Senior Citizens.* 1979 $7.95
Richard M. Bird	*The Growth of Public Employment in Canada.* 1979 $12.95
Richard Price (ed.)	*The Spirit of the Alberta Indian Treaties.* 1979 $8.95
Richard J. Schultz	*Federalism and the Regulatory Process.* 1979 $1.50
Richard J. Schultz	*Le fédéralisme et le processus de réglementation.* 1979 $1.50
Lionel D. Feldman & Katherine A. Graham	*Bargaining for Cities, Municipalities and Intergovernmental Relations: An Assessment.* 1979 $10.95
Elliot J. Feldman & Neil Nevitte (eds.)	*The Future of North America: Canada, the United States, and Quebec Nationalism.* 1979 $7.95
Pierre Sormany	*Les micro-esclaves : vers une bio-industrie canadienne.* 1979 $3.00
Maximo Halty-Carrere	*Technological Development Strategies for Developing Countries: A Review for Policy Makers.* 1979 $12.95
David R. Protheroe	*Imports and Politics: Trade Decision Making in Canada, 1968-1979.* 1980 $8.95
Zavis P. Zeman & David Hoffman (eds.)	*The Dynamics of the Technological Leadership of the World.* 1980 $3.00

G. Bruce Doern	*Government Intervention in the Canadian Nuclear Industry.* 1980 $8.95
G. Bruce Doern & Robert W. Morrison (eds.)	*Canadian Nuclear Policies.* 1980 $14.95
Russell Wilkins	*Health States in Canada, 1926-1976.* 1980 $3.00
Russell Wilkins	*L'état de santé au Canada, 1926-1976.* 1980 $3.00
Allan M. Maslove & Gene Swimmer	*Wage Controls in Canada: 1975-78: A Study of Public Decision Making.* 1980 $11.95
T. Gregory Kane	*Consumers and the Regulators: Intervention in the Federal Regulatory Process.* 1980 $10.95
Réjean Lachapelle & Jacques Henripin	*La situation démolinguistique au Canada: évolution passée et prospective.* 1980 $24.95
Albert Breton & Anthony Scott	*The Design of Federations.* 1980 $6.95
A.R. Bailey & D.G. Hull	*The Way Out: A More Revenue-Dependent Public Sector and How It Might Revitalize the Process of Governing.* 1980 $6.95
David R. Harvey	*Christmas Turkey or Prairie Vulture? An Economic Analysis of the Crow's Nest Pass Grain Rates.* 1980 $10.95
Donald G. Cartwright	*Official Language Populations in Canada: Patterns and Contacts.* 1980 $4.95
Richard M. Bird	*Taxing Corporations.* 1980 $6.95
Leroy O. Stone & Susan Fletcher	*A Profile of Canada's Older Population.* 1980 $7.95
Peter N. Nemetz (ed.)	*Resource Policy: International Perspectives.* 1980 $18.95
Keith A.J. Hay (ed.)	*Canadian Perspectives on Economic Relations With Japan.* 1980 $18.95
Dhiru Patel	*Dealing With Interracial Conflict: Policy Alternatives.* 1980 $5.95
Raymond Breton & Gail Grant	*La langue de travail au Québec : synthèse de la recherche sur la rencontre de deux langues.* 1981 $10.95

Diane Vanasse	*L'évolution de la population scolaire du Québec.* 1981 $12.95
David M. Cameron (ed.)	*Regionalism and Suparnationalism: Challenges and Alternatives to the Nation-State in Canada and Europe.* 1981 $9.95
Heather Menzies	*Women and the Chip: Case Studies of the Effects of Informatics on Employment in Canada.* 1981 $8.95
H.V. Kroeker (ed.)	*Sovereign People or Sovereign Governments.* 1981 $12.95
Peter Aucoin (ed.)	*The Politics and Management of Restraint in Government.* 1981 $17.95
Nicole S. Morgan	*Nowhere to Go? Possible Consequences of the Demographic Imbalance in Decision-Making Groups of the Federal Public Service.* 1981 $8.95
Nicole S. Morgan	*Où aller? Les conséquences prévisibles des déséquilibres démographiques chez les groupes de décision de la fonction publique fédérale.* 1981 $8.95
Raymond Breton, Jeffrey G. Reitz & Victor F. Valentine	*Les frontières culturelles et la cohésion du Canada.* 1981 $18.95
Peter N. Nemetz (ed.)	*Energy Crisis: Policy Response.* 1981 $18.95
James Gillies	*Where Business Fails.* 1981 $9.95
Robert A. Russel	*Office Automation: Key to the Information Society.* 1981 $3.00
Allan Tupper & G. Bruce Doern (eds.)	*Public Corporations and Public Policy in Canada.* 1981 $16.95
Réjean Lachapelle & Jacques Henripin	*The Demolinguistic Situation in Canada: Past Trends and Future Prospects.* 1982 $24.95
Irving Brecher	*Canada's Competition Policy Revisited: Some New Thoughts on an Old Story.* 1982 $3.00
Ian McAllister	*Regional Development and the European Community: A Canadian Perspective.* 1982 $13.95
Donald J. Daly	*Canada in an Uncertain World Economic Environment.* 1982 $3.00

| W.T. Stanbury & Fred Thompson | *Regulatory Reform in Canada.* 1982 $7.95 |

Robert J. Buchan, C. Christopher Johnston, T. Gregory Kane, Barry Lesser, Richard J. Schultz & W.T. Stanbury — *Telecommunications Regulation and the Constitution.* 1982 $18.95

Rodney de C. Grey — *United States Trade Policy Legislation: A Canadian View.* 1982 $7.95

John Quinn & Philip Slayton (eds.) — *Non-Tariff Barriers After the Tokyo Round.* 1982 $17.95

Stanley M. Beck & Ivan Bernier (eds.) — *Canada and the New Constitution: The Unfinished Agenda.* 2 vols. 1982 $10.95

R. Brian Woodrow & Kenneth B. Woodside (eds.) — *The Introduction of Pay-TV in Canada: Issues and Implications.* 1982 $14.95

E.P. Weeks & L. Mazany — *The Future of the Atlantic Fisheries.* 1983 $5.00

Douglas D. Purvis (ed.), assisted by Frances Chambers — *The Canadian Balance of Payments: Perspectives and Policy Issues.* 1983 $24.95

Roy A. Matthews — *Canada and the "Little Dragons": An Analysis of Economic Developments in Hong Kong, Taiwan, South Korea and the Challenge/Opportunity They Present for Canadian Interests in the 1980s.* 1983 $11.95

Charles F. Doran — *Economic Interdependence, Autonomy, and Canadian/American Relations.* 1983 $5.00

Charles Pearson & Gerry Salembier — *Trade, Employment, and Adjustment.* 1983 $5.00

Steven Globerman — *Cultural Regulation in Canada.* 1983 $11.95

F.R. Flatters & R.G. Lipsey — *Common Ground for the Canadian Common Market.* 1983 $5.00

Frank Bunn, assisted by U. Domb, D. Huntley, H. Mills, H. Silverstein — *Oceans from Space: Towards the Management of Our Coastal Zones.* 1983 $5.00

C.D. Shearing & P.C. Stenning — *Private Security and Private Justice: The Challenge of the 80s.* 1983 $5.00

Jacob Finkelman & Shirley B. Goldenberg	*Collective Bargaining in the Public Service: The Federal Experience in Canada.* 2 vols. 1983 $29.95
Gail Grant	*The Concrete Reserve: Corporate Programs for Indians in the Urban Work Place.* 1983 $5.00
Roy George	*Targeting High-Growth Industry.* 1983 $5.00
Owen Adams & Russell Wilkins	*Healthfulness of Life.* 1984 $5.00
Yoshi Tsurumi with Rebecca R. Tsurumi	*Sogoshosha: Engines of Export-Based Growth* (Revised Edition). 1984 $10.95
Raymond Breton & Gail Grant	*The Dynamics of Government Programs for Urban Indians in the Prairie Provinces.* 1984 $19.95
Frank Stone	*Canada, The GATT and the International Trade System.* 1984 $15.00
R.J. Wonnacott	*Aggressive U.S. Reciprocity Evaluated with a New Analytical Approach to Trade Conflict.* 1984 $8.00
R.J. Wonnacott	*Selected New Developments in International Trade Theory.* 1984 $7.00
Paul K. Gorecki & W.T. Stanbury	*The Objectives of Canadian Competition Policy, 1888-1983.* 1984 $15.00
Mark Thompson & Gene Swimmer	*Conflict or Compromise: The Future of Public Sector Industrial Relations.* 1984 $15.00
Pierre Sauvé	*Private Bank Lending and Developing-Country Debt.* 1984 $10.00
Richard W. Wright	*Japanese Business in Canada: The Elusive Alliance.* 1984 $12.00
Samuel Wex	*Instead of FIRA: Autonomy for Canadian Subsidiaries.* 1984 $8.00

---

*Order Address: The Institute for Research on Public Policy
P.O. Box 3670
Halifax, Nova Scotia
B3J 3K6